Success *guides*

D0998100

Standard Grade
Business Management

Derek McInally ✗ Anne Ross

Contents

Human Resources

Finance

Examination Advice

Standard Grade Business Management

Purpose of the guide

The purpose of this Success Guide is to support students who are undertaking Standard Grade Business Management. It is also hoped that this publication will be of help to the vast number of parents who are confused by the course structure and the assessment terminology used in Standard Grade.

There are many aspects of Standard Grade Business Management which are common to other Standard Grades, but there are techniques explained in this Success Guide which will assist students achieving their potential in Standard Grade Business Management.

A Success Guide could never hope to provide detailed coverage of the whole Standard Grade course, this was never the intention of the authors. This Success Guide will provide an insight into the main aspects of the Standard Grade course. First, the Practical Abilities project will be covered. This is normally sat in the latter stages of fourth year. Chapters 2 to 6 will cover the five main themes of the Standard Grade course. Those sections which refer only to Credit Level are highlighted. The final chapter will provide examination advice and useful tips on the final exam, covering the elements of Knowledge and Understanding (KU) and Decision Making (DM). A glossary has been provided at the end of this book to help with definitions of key terms.

Introduction

Standard Grade Business Management is a dynamic subject which is constantly evolving to reflect what is happening in the real world of business. This means that students of Business Management must make sure that they keep abreast of developments by reading quality newspapers and watching TV programmes which discuss current events in business.

Your overall mark will be based on a Practical Abilities project which you will normally undertake in January or February of your final year of study. The Scottish Qualification Authority (SQA) produces projects every year, and Chapter 1 of this book is dedicated to achieving success in Practical Abilities. There is also an external exam produced by the SQA covering Knowledge and Understand (KU) and Decision Making (DM).

Approximately 6500 candidates sit Standard Grade Business Management every year and it is important to realise that the vast majority of these pass. This Success Guide is about making sure that not only are you one of them, but that you also achieve your potential by being fully aware of what the examiners will be looking for in your examination scripts.

Your Standard Grade exams are likely to be the first major exams you have ever sat and almost certainly the first ones which will be marked by teachers outwith your school. The marker of your Standard Grade Business Management paper will not know you and so cannot give you the benefit of any doubt. It is therefore vital that you understand what is expected of you.

In the external exam, the Foundation paper lasts 1 hour; the General paper lasts 1 hour 15 minutes and the Credit exam lasts 1 hour 30 minutes. Roughly equal marks will be awarded for KU and DM questions. The format of each of the different levels is generally the same: stimulus material, or a short case study, and questions which will cover more than one area of the course. All the questions are compulsory so you cannot afford to miss out any part of the course.

Practice of the final examination paper is vital, and recent papers at General and Credit levels can be purchased from Leckie and Leckie.

The PA project

Business@work

The PA project involves the running of your own computer-simulated stationery business through a software package called business@work. Each year SQA produces projects at Foundation, General and Credit levels which test parts of the simulation.

You will have 15–20 hours to complete your project. You will submit only one project at either Foundation, General or Credit level. Because time is limited, it is important that you make sure you start the correct level.

Improving your grade

The PA project counts towards one third of your overall grade and this is an ideal way of increasing your final mark. Many students do better in the PA project than in the final exam. The reason for this is simple; the PA projects are not sat under strict time constraints and therefore you are not as pressurised. You have time to think about your answers, sometimes over several days, and so you can mull over answers and improve them. Another major factor is that some of the questions are KU or DM based and you are encouraged to use your notes and textbooks to answer them.

Your teacher marks these papers and checks are carried out by the SQA to ensure the correct standard is being met. Your teacher can provide guidance to you while sitting the project, but if you need too much help they will down-grade you to reflect the amount of support given.

The work submitted has to be your own. If it can be established that all, or even part of the work submitted for your project is significantly similar to another student, both of you will fail your Standard Grade Business Management, and it could lead to you being withdrawn from all your Standard Grades. Copying someone else's answers or allowing them to copy yours simply is not worth it.

Marks and grades

The PA papers are each made up of 60 marks. To achieve the upper grade, 1, 3 or 5, you must achieve over 75% in the relevant paper The lower grade, 2, 4 or 6 will be awarded to students who achieve 50% or more. If you narrowly fail the General or Credit level, you will be given a grade below. So, for example, if you sit the Credit paper and only get 24 marks, i.e. 40%, then you will be awarded a General level 3.

How the project is made up

The PA project is split into three sections:

- Section 1 tests your ability to make good use of the software program while working in business@work.
- Section 2 looks at particular areas of your stationery business and relates these to the Business Management course.
- Section 3 is a case study or stimulus material with questions on a real-life business enterprise.

Printouts

For each paper you will need to produce a minimum of two printouts that are meaningful to the activities or tasks. One mark will be awarded for each printout. The timing of printouts is crucial. Go too far in the simulation and you might be unable to print out the desired page; so read through the whole paper before you start and plan your printouts. Additional marks can be awarded at General level if you highlight aspects of the printout, while at Credit level you will be expected to make comments or compare printouts.

Top Tip

Plan when you need to print. Trading and Profit and Loss Account and Balance Sheets are calculated every quarter (ie every 3 months) during the simulation. When you move from one quarter to the next you cannot retrieve the previous quarters figures.

Quick Test

1 How many hours will you be given to complete the Practical Abilities (PA) project?

2 How much does the Practical Abilities (PA) element count towards the final award in SG Business Management?

3 What percentage is necessary to achieve the upper grade in a project ie grades 1, 3 or 5?

4 State the percentage necessary to achieve the lower grade ie grades 2, 4 or 6.

5 If you score between 40-49% in the Credit project can you still get a grade?

Answers 1. 15-20 hours 2. One-third 3. 75% or over 4. Between 50-74% 5. Yes, General Grade 3

Business@work – the simulation

Setting the scene

You are asked to imagine that you have recently bought a stationery and printing business from Marie Lucas. Although the business does not come with any premises or staff, Marie sells you some equipment and provides you with some start-up advice.

You run your business in the make-believe town of Mereside, which has 200,000 inhabitants. As well as being a busy industrial centre, the town of Mereside is a popular tourist destination with its own castle.

Most of your business decisions will revolve around your office where you are expected to work through a number of tasks before running your business for 12 months.

Cash flow and profit or losses will be automatically calculated for you and will be based on the decisions you make.

To gain access to the simulation your teacher needs to provide you with a password, instruction on how to locate the software and where to save your decisions.

Getting started

The first time you load business@work, begin by running through the demo. This is found by clicking on the top quadrant of the opening diamond.

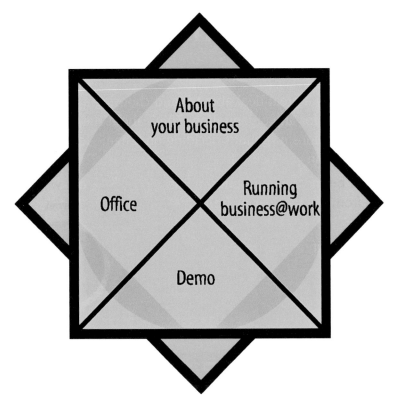

Most of the tools you will require for business@work can be accessed by directly clicking on them in your new office or by clicking on the   icon on the tool bar at the bottom of your screen.

The demo can be used to provide details of all aspects of your office, or you can select individual icons to inform you of one or more aspect of the simulation. While in the demo you can pause if it is going too fast, return to the demo menu or quit demo by clicking on your choice from the tool bar at the bottom of your screen.

While in demo menu all other icons at the bottom of the screen are deactivated.

The simulation involves the completion of 11 tasks from a 'to-do' list. Each time a task is completed a 'smiling face' appears next to the task on the to-do list to indicate that it has been completed.

Top Tip
Generally you must complete each task in the order they appear on the to-do list, but it is possible to undertake the recruitment tasks (tasks 6–10) at any stage.
At the end of the simulation you must print your to-do list as this is required by the SQA as proof that you have completed business@work.

The to-do list (Tasks 1–3)

Task 1 Choose a name for your business

The name of a business can say a great deal about it and choosing a good one can be the start of success for any organisation. Think about the many companies that have spent millions of pounds deciding on a name for their business or those who have changed their names.

Find out about choosing a business name from the Business Works.com website. The Internet is accessed from the tool bar or from the PC in your office.

Internet

You should be prepared to justify your choice of name, so give it some serious thought.

Task 2 Choose a site for your business

This is perhaps one of the most important decisions for a business. Not only will it affect the volume of sales, but it will also directly affect costs as well as operations.

Start your research by finding out about the location from the hyperlink on your Internet homepage.

The map provides lots of background information about Mereside and the commercial sites available for rent. The map is accessed either from the office wall or from the tool bar.

Top Tip
Use the Personal Digital Assistant (PDA) to make notes on each of the four properties available for rent.

Take time to watch and listen to each of the video clips which provide useful background information to the town of Mereside.

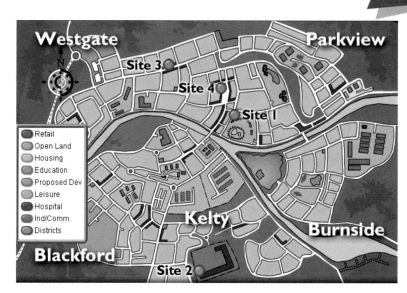

Westgate Parkview

Site 3
Site 4
Site 1

Retail
Open Land
Housing
Education
Proposed Dev
Leisure
Hospital
Ind/Comm.
Districts

Kelty Burnside

Blackford

Site 2

You will be able to view each of the available four sites by simply clicking on the site number. You can then find out more information by continuing to click on each of the sites.

Once you visit a site, financial information will automatically be transferred to the site planner on your PC. This will allow you to make direct comparisons regarding rent, alterations and loans required.

The start-up file provided by Marie Lucas suggests that your loan should be between £5000 and £6000. Only Site 1 meets this criterion. The advice on the size of the loan is only a suggestion and you are free to disregard it.

Whether you go for Site 1, 2, 3 or 4, you must justify your decision.

Site Planner

Start-up file

Task 3 Do some market research

Market research can make or break a new venture like your stationery and printing business. The Internet will provide background knowledge and understanding on marketing and research. Take time to read this information, it is also good revision for your final examination.

Top Tip

Market research is money well spent.
You have the choice of selecting answers to four questions at a cost of £50 each. The answers to these questions will be found on the main menu of your PC and will support you in future decisions.
You will be asked to give a reason for your choice of market research questions.

Quick Test

1. Name the town where your business is located.
2. Who did you buy the business from?
3. List the five districts of the town.
4. What advice are you given on the size of bank loan?
5. How much does each market research question cost?

Answers 1. Mereside **2.** Marie Lucas **3.** Westgate, Parkview, Burnside, Kelty, and Blackford **4.** Between £5000 and £6000 **5.** £50

The to-do list (Tasks 4–5)

This task will take you the most time and will require information on your business from the start-up lever arch file provided by Marie Lucas. You can also find out general information about a business plan by using the search function on the Business Works.com website.

Some entries in the business plan have already been transferred for you, such as the equipment purchased from Marie Lucas, the name of your business and the amount spent on market research – these cannot be altered. Other information, such as the site chosen and monthly rent, is also entered but this can be changed in the business plan.

Production Planner

Use your production planner on your PC to decide on your selling price. Marie claims that a price of £2.89 will result in most of your products being sold. Remember this is only a suggestion and your price can be anything from £2.49 to £3.99 for non-contract sales.

The production planner should also be used to calculate production levels. In general it can be argued that paying staff overtime should be avoided as this pushes up costs. This will limit non-contract sales to 2400 units in the early months. However, many successful entrepreneurs will claim overtime is necessary to ensure adequate levels of production to meet demand and thus generate income.

Note that the production rate rises after month 2 from 20 units per hour to 25 units per hour.

The rise in production rate in month 3 is due to increased efficiency by your workers as experience makes them more skilled in carrying out their work.

Top Tip
Use the calculator function on your PDA to work out running costs.

When calculating the monthly sales figures, take some account of potential changes in non-contract demand for your products. As a general example, ice cream sales are higher in the summer when it is hot, and at Christmas when there are children's parties, than at other times of the year. Consider when your peak times are likely to be.

When working out the monthly running costs, the easiest way is simply to divide the annual cost of each expense by 12. This is the way that most businesses pay for things like electricity, as it smoothes out fluctuating costs.

When you complete this task the smiling face symbol at the side will initially appear a lighter shade than the previous ones. This indicates that the business plan can be altered. However, be aware that every time you alter the business plan you must also redo Task 5 before you can continue. This can be time-consuming and is best avoided.

TO DO LIST

☺ 1 Choose a name for your business
☺ 2 Choose a site for your business
☺ 3 Do market research
☺ 4 Prepare a Business Plan
   5 Meet your Bank Manager

Task 5 Meet your bank manager

In order to obtain a loan necessary to start your business you are required to answer three questions set by your bank manager. These questions will vary from one student to the next and so are unpredictable. In general, they require a great deal of thought and you would be advised to use your Business Management course notes to answer them thoroughly. Remember there is less pressure for you to answer quickly, so consider researching each of the questions one by one.

The bank manager will decide whether to give you a loan, based not only on your answers to the questions but also on the financial information generated by business@work. If a loan is not approved then you will be required to change the entries in your business plan and revisit the bank manager.

Top Tip
If you save and quit the scenario there is no guarantee that when you return to complete Task 5 the bank manager will ask you the same questions.

Quick Test

1. Where in business@work can you find information on your business?
2. Which tool will help decide on a selling price?
3. Why does the production rate rise after month 2?
4. How many questions will the bank manager ask you?
5. If the loan is not approved, where will you have to make changes?

Answers 1. Start up lever-arch file **2.** Production planner **3.** Workers become more skilled **4.** 3 **5.** Business plan

The to-do list (Tasks 6–11)

Task 6 Prepare job descriptions and person specifications

Your start-up lever arch file will provide information about future employees, and following the recruitment hyperlink on the Business Works.com website will provide details and examples of job descriptions and person specifications.

You need to appoint an administration assistant and a production assistant for your business. You will be asked for reasons for your choice of items for the job description for your administration assistant, so choose sensibly.

Note that when you identify three items for the person specifications under 'essential', the desirable ones are automatically selected.

Task 7 Advertising your administration vacancy

You are required to justify one of the items selected for inclusion in your advertisement for the administration assistant. You will then receive applications in your office in and out tray from seven people applying for the post of production assistant and eight applying for the post of administration assistant. Open each of these letters and read the applications.

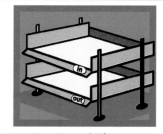

Task 8 Interview and choose your production assistant

Once you start the interview process you cannot return to the office to read the letters so make sure you have taken adequate notes. Follow the hyperlinks on 'who to interview' found under recruitment. You might find it useful to print off copies of the interview checklist for use during the interview process.

Top Tip
Use your PDA to make notes on each of the applicants. When adding notes to your PDA, type over <new> with a file name so that you can find them again.

Task 9 Interview and choose your administration assistant

You will be asked to give a reason why you have selected one of your applicants for the post of administration assistant. You will also have to say why you have chosen one of the questions selected for use during the interview. Finally you must give a reason for choosing the successful applicant.

Task 10 Write letters to successful and unsuccessful applicants

Here you are required to decide on the format of the letters to be sent to the successful candidates and also the letter which will go to the unsuccessful candidates.

You will choose from a number of standard phrases. These letters are important so think carefully why you are selecting each statement.

Task 11 Run your business simulation

Top Tip
When you attempt to leave business@work the program will prompt you to save your work. The only way not to save your decisions is to switch off the power!

You will now run your business for the next 12 months. Once you start on the simulation you cannot alter your business plan.

For each month of the simulation check your cash budget. Marie suggests that you keep a cash balance of £1800 each month. Check your trading, profit and loss account each quarter to see what effect your decisions are having on your business. You can view and print your financial accounts from the PC.

Throughout the simulation you are asked to state the amount you wish to spend on market research. A reason is expected. The amount you spend on advertising can also be adjusted.

Use your production planner from your PC to make decisions on estimated production levels. Production on non-contract goods must be greater than 1800 units with selling prices between £2.49 and £3.99. This will result in a monthly income greater than £3900.

Shocks are reported throughout the simulation indicating potential changes in demand or production levels. There is nothing you can do to prevent these.

E-mail

You will receive two emails during the simulation. These will appear initially as red envelopes on the tool bar. You may also access your emails via the PC. You should read your emails and take corresponding action.

Quick Test

1. Name two places you can find information on recruitment in business@work.
2. State the job titles of the staff you intend to employ.
3. How are you going to attract applicants for the posts?
4. Which form will you find useful when interviewing candidates?
5. How do you inform candidates if they have been successful or unsuccessful in their interview?

Answers 1. Start-up lever arch file and Business Works.com website **2.** Administration assistant and production assistant **3.** Advertise **4.** Interview checklist **5.** Letter

Tool bar summary

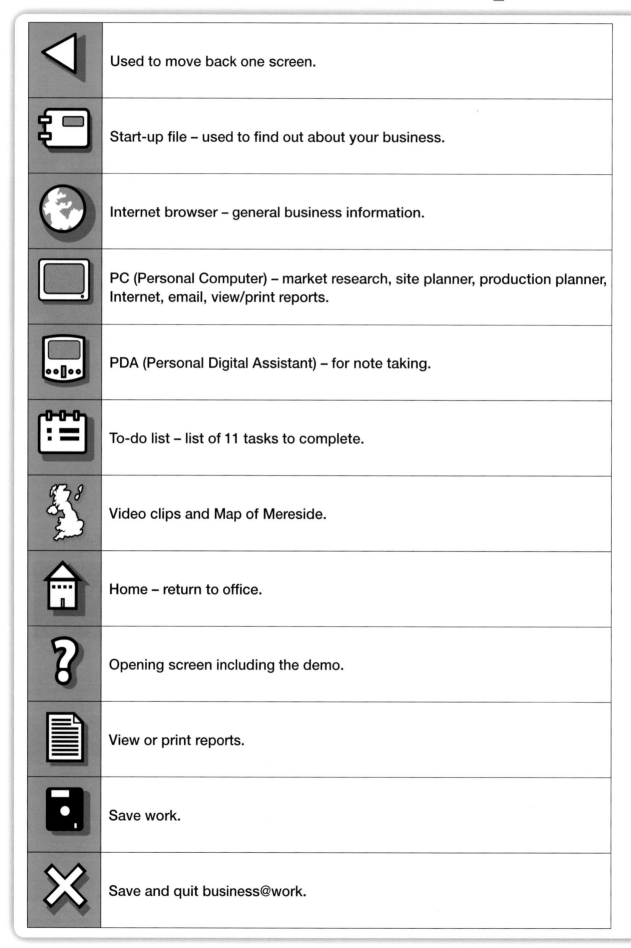	Used to move back one screen.
	Start-up file – used to find out about your business.
	Internet browser – general business information.
	PC (Personal Computer) – market research, site planner, production planner, Internet, email, view/print reports.
	PDA (Personal Digital Assistant) – for note taking.
	To-do list – list of 11 tasks to complete.
	Video clips and Map of Mereside.
	Home – return to office.
	Opening screen including the demo.
	View or print reports.
	Save work.
	Save and quit business@work.

The SQA Practical Abilities examination

The PA paper set by SQA is made up of three sections and takes the form of a report.

Section 1 of business@work

This section tests your ability to use the software. It asks you direct questions on the use of the various tools used in the simulation, such as the Personal Digital Assistant (PDA) or one or more of the programs on your PC.

Foundation question

Question:	**Marks**
Below is your office from business@work. State how you access the Personal Digital Assistant.	2

Answer:

Click on the PDA on the office desk. 1 mark

Click on the PDA icon on the tool bar. 1 mark

General question

Question:	Marks
During business@work you should have used the Personal Digital Assistant (PDA) shown below.	2

(i) Did you find the PDA useful? Tick (✓) your answer.

Yes	
No	

(ii) Explain your choice.

No, it kept blocking the screen when opened 1 mark

No because I could not print my notes 1 mark

or

Yes, it allowed me to organise my notes. 1 mark

Yes because it helped me keeps notes 1 mark

Answer:

Top Tip
There are no marks for your choice of yes or no. Marks are only awarded for your explanation.

Credit question

Question:	Marks
Discuss limitations of the PDA during business@work.	2

Pages cannot be stored in folders, resulting in loss of data. 1 mark

The PDA cannot print. 1 mark

Answer:

Top Tip
When completing the Credit project it is a good idea to type your answers. Use double-line spacing. This allows you to go back and amend answers.

Section 2 of business@work

This section looks in more detail about particular aspects of the business, such as recruitment or location.

In exam questions, Foundation pupils are asked much more to *identify*, *name*, *state*, *give examples*, *match* or *complete*, while General pupils are more likely to be asked to *describe*, *recommend* or *suggest*, and Credit pupils will need to demonstrate greater knowledge with *explain*, *discuss* or *justify*. There is a degree of overlap in the use of terminology between levels and what will determine the level is the depth of your answer.

Section 2 will normally contain the questions which ask for printouts. Each page of information can be printed or simply viewed from the PC by clicking on view/print reports.

The following menu will appear:

Top Tip

All of the decisions you make are recorded automatically in the player's workbook. Decisions made in the business plan can be printed, as can financial information.

Reports

- Player's Workbook
- Business Plan
- Cash Budget
- Trading and Profit and Loss Account
- Balance Sheet
- To do Status

To print all data simply click on the print icon. If only one page is needed select the view icon, find the page and then print.

Top Tip

A cash budget is available for each month based on the figures you have inserted. The trading and profit and loss and balance sheet are available as forecasts before the simulation and then every quarter until the end of the simulated year.

Note that this is where the to-do list will be printed for final submission with your project.

At General and Credit level, Section 2 will contain questions which require you to demonstrate the ability to deal with a number of pieces of information (at General level normally in the format of a table). These questions often attract a high number of marks.

Foundation question

Question:

Use your site planner to complete the following table.

Marks 4

Site	Rent
1	
2	
3	
4	

Answer

Site	Rent	
1	£625	1 mark
2	£900	1 mark
3	£1000	1 mark
4	£1100	1 mark

General question

Question:

Marie Lucas suggests that your loan should be between £5000 and £6000.
Only Site 1 satisfies this criteria.
Other than the size of the loan, suggest two other advantages of Site 1.

Marks 2

Advantage 1 ....

Advantage 2 ....

Answer:

Advantage 1 ....Situated in the town centre, busy location.......... 1 mark

Advantage 2 ....Good car parking nearby for customers and deliveries.... 1 mark

Credit question

Question:

Compare Site 1 with Sites 2–4.

Marks 2

Answer:

Site 1 has the cheapest rent at £625 per month. 1 mark

Sites 2–4 all have good parking but Site 1 has limited parking spaces. 1 mark

Section 3 of business@work

This section includes a case study or stimulus material on a real life business or enterprise. Part of the purpose of this section is to test you on another business and also prepare you for the final paper where questions have a short case study attached to them.

The following stimulus material or case study relates to the questions which follow.

For over 30 years The Prince's Scottish Youth Business Trust has supported young people in Scotland to realise their ambition to be entrepreneurs and set up their own business. The Prince's Trust is a registered charity and has helped over half a million people – that is the same as the entire population of Edinburgh.

Unemployed people aged between 18–25, who have an idea for a business but can't raise all the cash needed from anywhere else, can get help from the Trust.

With start-up support from The Prince's Scottish Youth Business Trust, a young person could get:

- a low interest loan of up to £4000 for a sole trader, or up to £5000 for a partnership
- a grant of up to £1000
- a test marketing grant of up to £250
- ongoing advice from a volunteer business mentor
- access to a wide range of goods and services including a free legal helpline.

Source: www.princes-trust.org.uk

Question:	Marks
Tick (✓) the type of business your stationery business is:	1

Sole trader	
Partnership	

Answer:

Sole trader	✓	1 mark
Partnership		

Exam style question

Question:	Marks
Suggest two benefits of a grant over a loan in setting up your stationery business.	2

Answer:

A grant does not need to be paid back. 1 mark

A loan will often have interest added to it. 1 mark

Question:	Marks
Other than The Prince's Scottish Youth Trust, suggest and justify additional sources of advice for your business.	6

Answer:

The bank manager – they have lots of experience of new businesses. 2 marks

Your Business Management teacher – they are on hand. 2 marks

Business Gateway – they are set up by the Government specifically to support new businesses. 2 marks

CREDIT

The market

Marketing

An organisation might have its own marketing department, but whether or not they do, all organisations, either in the public or private sectors, carry out marketing activities – so this topic is important.

A market

A market is where customers and sellers exchange goods and services for money. It can be a local market (limited to a small area); a national market (involving buyers and sellers throughout the country) or an international market (where buyers and sellers come from different countries).

Some markets are direct. These involve customers and sellers meeting face-to-face, such as in a shop or at an ice-cream van. Another type of market is where the buyer and seller do not physically meet, such as buying through mail order, over the Internet or via a TV shopping channel.

Marketing answers the what, who, why and where questions:

- What are we going to sell or provide?
- Who are we going to sell it to?
- Why will they buy our goods or services?
- Where will we provide it to gain maximum sales?

What are you going to sell?

The term entrepreneur is the name given to a person who develops a business idea. There are lots of famous Scottish entrepreneurs. Sir Alexander Fleming, who was born in Ayrshire, discovered the drug penicillin. More recently, Michelle Mone from Glasgow has made a fortune from the design and manufacture of ladies' lingerie. Entrepreneurs are not only responsible for coming up with an idea, they also see it through to the point where customers want the goods or service, and can easily get hold of it.

What customers want can best be answered through market research. This is the process of gathering and analysing or studying information to help a business become successful.

Top Tip
Use a search engine to find out more about Scottish entrepreneurs like Fleming and Mone.

Quick Test

1 What is a market?

2 Describe the meaning of an international market.

3 Give an example of a direct market.

4 What is an entrepreneur?

5 Give examples of entrepreneurs in your local area.

Market research

There are two types of market research.

Field research

Information is gathered either by yourself or a market research company. Field Research is also known as primary information

Advantages of field research:

- The information gathered will be relevant to your needs.

- Because you have just collected it, it is up-to-date.

- You know how reliable it is because you have been involved in its collection.

Top Tip
When asked for advantages, do not simply say quick, easy, cheap. You must relate these terms to something, e.g. quicker than ... easier because ...

Methods of field research include the following:

Questionnaire/survey: Information is gathered by asking questions and recording the answers. This can take place face-to-face with someone in the street, by phone, by post, over the Internet or via interactive television. Information gathered by questionnaire is recorded and so can be easily referred back to. The major problem with questionnaires is people are reluctant to complete them, so return rates are often low.

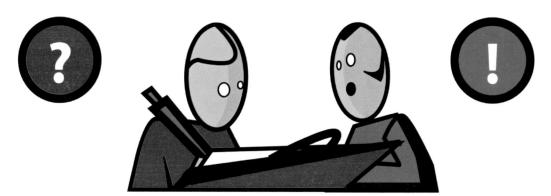

Consumer panel: A group of customers are brought together and asked to discuss a product. Because they actually use the item their feedback can be relevant. However, these are customers who use the product, and as such you are not finding out what people who do not use the product think.

Hall test: A group of people, not necessary current consumers, are brought together and asked for their opinion on a good or service. This information tends to be accurate, but it might prove difficult to get a cross section of the public, so findings might not be complete.

Product test: Members of the public are asked to use a product for a period of time and then asked questions at the end of the trial. This tests customer reactions over a period of time and therefore is relevant. However, such testing is very time consuming.

Desk research

Information has previously been collected for one purpose and is used by you for another. It already exists. This second hand information is also called secondary information.

Top Tip
When asked for the disadvantages of desk research, you can compare them to the advantages of field research.

Advantages of desk research

- Because it has already been collected it is easier to obtain than field research.
- The ease by which it can be collected often makes it quicker to obtain.
- Information which is already there is cheaper to gather.

Not all information is of use. For information to be of value it must be timely, accurate, relevant, cost effective and complete.

Methods of desk research include the following:

Financial reports: The accounts of an organisation tell you a great deal about the success of that organisation and you can use either your own accounts or those of competitors. Financial reports are often readily available and so are cost-effective. However, accounts measure money and do not reflect non-financial assets such as staff morale or how good the managers are.

Government publications: The government publishes lots of useful information such as the Census of Population which can help a business decide where to set up trading. These publications are easily accessible and are often on the Internet. They also tend to be accurate. However, they take so long to produce they are often out-of-date by the time they are published.

General publications: These are available to anyone and include magazines, trade journals and phone directories. They are readily available and are cost effective, but if competitors are writing about themselves they often only provide positive information.

Carrying out market research will provide organisations with an insight into the minds of customers. From the information obtained they will be able to devise a plan to satisfy needs and wants. Businesses will be able to plan how best to use their limited resources to achieve their objectives.

When a business manages to provide something no one else does then it has a **competitive advantage**.

Quick Test

1. Describe the purpose of **Market Research**.
2. Name the two types of Market Research?
3. What does information have to be if it is of value?
4. Suggest three methods of carrying out market research.

Answers 1. To find out what customers want. **2.** field and desk **3.** Timely, accurate, relevant, cost effective and complete **4.** Three of the following: questionnaire/surveys, customer panel, hall test, product test, compare financial reports

Who are your customers?

Market segmentation

The market for a good or service can be divided into groups of people who have common characteristics. This is known as market segmentation. It is important to know who your customers are and what their habits are, so you know how to get their attention.

The main ways the market can be segmented are described below.

Age

Businesses often target people of a particular age. There are magazines that are aimed at younger people such as *Bliss* with stories and articles which teenagers find interesting. Magazines like *Woman's Own* have articles for older readers.

Top Tip

Sometimes the person who buys the product or service is not the end user (consumer). Businesses have to take account of this when advertising products. As an example, when a business advertises flowers for Mothers' Day – it does not aim the advert at Mothers!

Gender

Businesses will sometimes aim their product at a particular gender. This may be because market research has shown that normally it is males or females who prefer their product and so they do not want to waste resources. Examples of this would be perfume or aftershave.

Social class

Consumers can be divided into different social classes. This allows organisations to target a particular group.

One way of grouping people is as follows:

A	Upper class
B	Middle class
C1	Upper working class
C2	Working class
D	Unskilled workers
E	Low paid/unemployed/ pensioners

Examples might be the readers of the *Sun* (social classes D or C2) and the *Scotsman* (social class B).

Income

This is similar to social class where people who earn more money can be persuaded to buy one product over another. For example, luxury holidays will be marketed to high earners.

CREDIT

Geography

People from different areas sometimes want different things. If you live in a rural area you might want a four-wheel-drive car to get around. In the city a smaller car will be easier to park.

Family structure

Manufacturers are quick to discover that certain products will appeal to people with children or to people who live on their own. In supermarkets you can buy 'family sizes' packs or 'meals for one'.

Top Tip
Market segmentation identifies a general preference from practical groups. There will always be exceptions.

Identifying which market segment your customers come from is not a guarantee to success; but it will help an organisation to target its limited resources more effectively. A successful business is one that plans its activities, and part of this process is to know who your customers are.

Age

Gender

Social Class

Income

Geography

Family Structure

Quick Test

1. Suggest a good or service which might appeal to an older person?

2. Suggest a service that might appeal to a woman.

3. Which type of music might someone from Social Class A or B listen to?

4. What type of shoes would people from rural areas buy?

Answers 1. A walk-in bath, false teeth, insurance, bus tour, etc. **2.** A beautician, hairdresser, etc. **3.** Classical, opera, etc. **4.** Walking boots, wellingtons, etc.

The marketing mix – product

The marketing mix is the name given to the four Ps in marketing. They are: **P**roduct, **P**rice, **P**romotion and **P**lace. How these different elements are used in a business largely determine the why and where questions.

Product

The product is the actual item or service that you are providing. The usefulness and the quality are central to why someone will purchase it. This part of the marketing mix also involves the name given to the product and the packaging.

The life of a product or service is shown by the product life cycle. This charts the life of the product until it is withdrawn from the market.

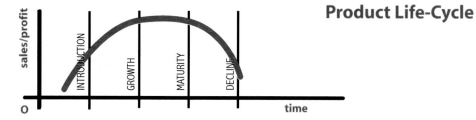

Product Life-Cycle

Stage 1 **Introduction**: This period is where sales and profits are low because few people know about the product. Demand is low.

Stage 2 **Growth**: During this stage sales and profits pick up. The product becomes more and more popular. Demand increases rapidly.

Stage 3 **Maturity**: At this point the product achieves maximum sales and profit levels. This is where the product has its greatest demand. From this point the fortunes of the product are likely to change.

Stage 4 **Decline**: Sales and profits fall off sharply as either competitors produce a better product or the public simply lose interest in it.

The shape of the product life cycle is true for all goods and services, although the steepness of curve does vary, and not all products reach all stages.

The product life cycle can be extended. This will prolong the life of the good or service.

Once a product reaches maturity, a manufacturer can watch it go into decline, or attempt to prolong its life. There are several ways in which the product life cycle can be extended. Changing the product slightly to include more features, changing the name, changing the price, even changing the use of the product are all ways in which new life can be brought into a good or service.

Top Tip
Maturity is sometimes called the saturation point, as competitors flood the market.

Top Tip
To extend the product life cycle of Mars bars, Mars increased their advertising, changed the recipe to make it lighter, gave it a new slogan and altered the packaging. They also developed spin offs such as Mars ice cream, Mars muffins and Mars drinks.

Product development

Because all products have a limited period of life it is normal for businesses to attempt to improve their existing products or launch new ones. This is known as product development.

Market led or product led?

A market led business makes real efforts to find out what the market wants before making a good or service. Some businesses are so confident in their product that they concentrate their efforts on simply ensuring the item for sale is the best it can be. This is known as product led.

Research and development (R&D)

Because all products will eventually go into decline it is important that organisations continue to develop new products to replace those which are losing profit. This process is called research and development (R&D). When a product is first developed it is called a prototype. Tests will be carried out to make sure the new product is safe and fit for purpose. Only when the product has been further refined will it be ready to be launched onto the market.

The creation of a PORTFOLIO, or group of products, can be useful if they are at different stages of the Product Life Cycle. One product at MATURITY will support a new product in INTRODUCTION and a product in GROWTH can support a product which is in DECLINE while searching for ways of extending its Product Life Cycle.

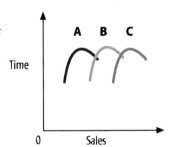

Quick Test

1 Name the 4Ps in the Marketing Mix.

2 State 4 stages of the Product Life Cycle.

3 At what stage of the Product Life Cycle are sales and profit levels at their highest?

4 Suggest one way of extending the Production Life Cycle.

5 What is the process called where businesses develop new products?

Answers 1. Product, Price, Promotion and Place **2.** Introduction, Growth, Maturity and Decline **3.** Maturity **4.** Alter the product, include more features, change the name, change the price or change the use of the product **5.** Research and Development (R&D)

The marketing mix – price

The price is the amount the good or service will be offered at to the customer. It can be used to explain why a customer buys it.

In general, a rise in price will normally result in fewer sales. However, sometimes people associate price with quality, so raising the price can result in an increase in demand.

Top Tip
In the exam, when suggesting a rise or fall in price, always justify why it will increase sales.

Introductory pricing

With introductory pricing the price is set low to encourage customers to try the product.

This is a temporary pricing structure. As popularity increases so does the price.

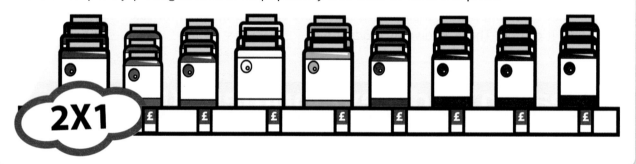

Loss leader

Here prices are set lower than costs. This pricing strategy might seem daft as the business will make a loss on each item that they sell but it is used to encourage customers to buy other things at the same time – earning the business profit.

Supermarkets make products such as bread and milk **loss leaders** to encourage customers to buy all their other groceries from them.

Penetrating pricing

This is where the organisation sets the price low to get a foothold in a competitive market. Once they have established themselves and secured loyalty they can raise the price.

Competitive pricing

This is where the price set is roughly the same as the other sellers in the market. This is normally the price adopted in markets where the goods are very similar or homogeneous.

Cost plus/mark-up

Here the supplier calculates the costs of providing the product and adds a bit on top, normally a percentage, to earn a profit.

Top Tip
Some pricing strategies can only be used for a short period such as Introductory, Penetrating, Skimming and Destroyer. Competitive, Cost Plus, Discriminatory and even Loss Leader pricing can be long term strategies.

Skimming

This pricing strategy is when a very high price is set to cream-off as much profit as possible. This can only work where there is not a lot of competition and where the product is in demand.

Destroyer pricing

This pricing structure is a low price strategy aimed at 'destroying' the competition by forcing them to go out of business. The business charges such a low price that no one can make a profit and so weaker businesses cannot survive. This can only be used when a business has more money to cover losses than their competitors.

Discriminatory pricing

This pricing strategy charges different prices to different people depending upon demand.

For example, holidays are much more expensive during the summer because it is a more popular time.

Quick Test

Name the pricing strategy that would be used in the following situations:

1. Low price strategy attempting to eliminate competition.
2. High price strategy where there is little or no competition.
3. Temporary low pricing strategy to encourage customers to try a new product.
4. Charging different customers different prices depending upon demand
5. Setting price to be the same as competition.
6. Where a percentage is added to costs.

Answers 1. Destroyer 2. Skimming 3. Introductory 4. Discriminatory 5. Competitive 6. Cost plus/mark up

The marketing mix – promotion

Promotion is the process by which people are encouraged to buy your product, rather than that of a competitor.

Advertising

Advertising is the major way in which companies will promote their good or service.

The different methods of advertising are discussed below.

- **Television:** Most people watch TV and therefore will find it hard to avoid adverts. Adverts can be seen between programmes, especially if a TV programme is sponsored by a particular product. You can even see adverts in TV programmes. This is called a placement, and it happens when certain products are used in programmes to encourage people to buy them.

The major advantage of TV advertising is it reaches such a wide audience, but the cost of advertising on TV, particularly at peak times, can be extortionate. Many people also switch over when the adverts come on.

- **Radio:** Radio stations will all advertise to some extent. The BBC advertises concerts, future radio shows and even TV programmes. Commercial radio stations only survive through the revenue generated from advertising between playing music.

Specialist radio stations can target specific segments of the market. For example, there are radio stations for young people and different shows for older people. A major disadvantage of using the radio to advertise is that people cannot see the good or service you are trying to sell and so rely on a description.

- **Cinema:** There has been a recent growth in the number of people attending the cinema and this has led to a growth in this type of advertising.

In the cinema people cannot switch to another channel, and the type of film can be used to target a particular segment. A disadvantage is the cost of making an advert for the cinema.

- **Posters/billboards:** Posters appear everywhere, from the side of roads to the side of buses.

Posters are around for a while, unlike a TV advert which only lasts a few seconds. Messages do however have to be short because people have a short time to look at them.

- **The Internet:** There are a growing number of companies who are choosing to use the Internet to advertise their products.

Adverts reach a large number of people but pop-up adverts can be blocked.

- **Sponsorship/endorsement:** This is where a company will advertise their name at a pop concert or, for example, on football shirts.

This can be very effective in building a recognisable name, but it can also put some people off if they do not like the football team.

Other promotion methods

Advertising is only one way to encourage people to buy your product. There are lots of other promotional techniques.

- **Competitions:** Some manufacturers will offer you the chance of taking part in a competition if you buy their product.
- **Free offers:** Free gifts will often encourage people to buy.
- **Buy One Get One Free (BOGOF):** This is a common way to encourage people to spend their money. This also includes special deals where you get a percentage free.
- **Money off coupons:** This can encourage someone to try a product if they get the coupon from a magazine or keep buying it if it is attached to the product.

Top Tip
Don't forget that advertising is not the only way to promote your product.

Branding

A brand is something that people recognise. The creation of a brand is used to make a product stand out from the rest. It can be the use of a name, colour, slogan or some unique aspect of design. Dyson is a good example of a brand. They make their vacuum cleaners and washing machines stand out from the rest with distinctive colours.

Examples of successful branding include Hoover, Sellotape and Tipp-Ex, where the name is so well known it is often used to describe a whole range of products.

The reason for creating a brand is to give the impression of quality or value-for-money which usually leads to loyalty. This can make it easier for a business to charge a higher price for their product. It might also make it easier to introduce a new product onto the market since people will already have heard, and possibly trust, the name.

The marketing mix – place

Place describes how the customer gains access to the good or service. A great product, at a good price, which is well promoted will still be unsuccessful unless the customer can get hold of it. The traditional way to buy a product is through a shop, but with the growth of e-commerce, increasing numbers of transactions are now carried out over the Internet.

Channel of distribution

The channel of distribution for a product is the way that it is sold to customers. The main options are shown below.

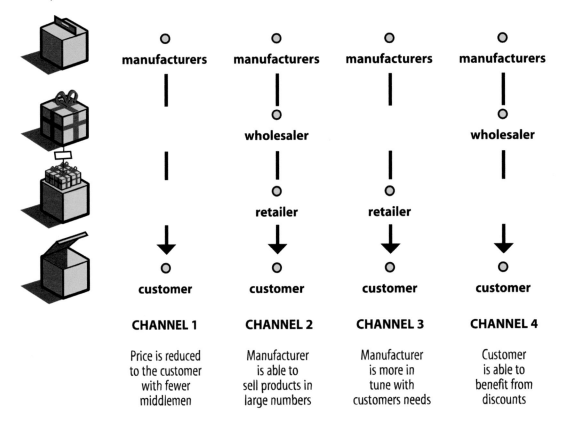

CHANNEL 1	CHANNEL 2	CHANNEL 3	CHANNEL 4
Price is reduced to the customer with fewer middlemen	Manufacturer is able to sell products in large numbers	Manufacturer is more in tune with customers needs	Customer is able to benefit from discounts

Some products can be distributed in a number of ways, for example, strawberries.

In the summer the farmer can sell direct to the customer at a Farmer's Market (Channel 1). Traditionally most farmers will sell to a wholesaler, who in turn will sell to a number of retail outlets/shops where customers will buy their strawberries (Channel 2). Larger retailers, such as Tesco, will miss out the wholesaler all together and purchase direct from the farmer before selling to the customer (Channel 3). Some wholesalers invite members of the public to purchase direct from them (Channel 4) such as at a fruit and vegetable wholesaler.

Method of distribution

The method of distribution for a product is the way that it is transported to its channel of distribution. The main options available are road, rail, sea or air. Which method is used will depend largely on the product. Items that are perishable (go off) such as dairy products will have to be transported quickly to market. Small items can go by a more expensive method because they do not take up much room.

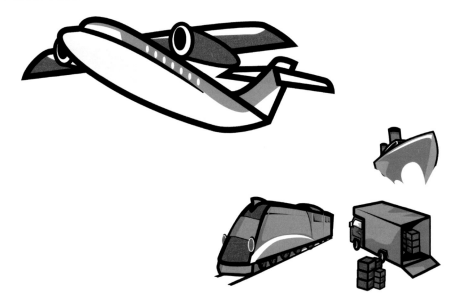

Marketing mix

The MARKETING MIX is the way in which the 4Ps are combined to produce best results. They are interrelated. Consideration must be taken of the effect each element of the Marketing Mix will have on the other. As an example, a high price strategy (PRICE) would not work if you decided to sell your product in a Discount Store (PLACE).

Top Tip

When attempting to increase the Product Life Cycle you must alter one or more of the 4Ps.

Quick Test

1. E-commerce has changed the way some products get to customers. How are more and more customers buying from businesses?

2. Which channel of distribution results in small amounts of goods being sold at one time by the manufacturer?

3. Describe the channel of distribution preferred by large retailers like Tesco.

4. Which method of distribution is likely to be the most expensive when transporting heavy goods large distances?

Answers 1. Via the Internet **2.** Manufacturer direct to customer **3.** Manufacturer to retailer to customer **4.** Air

Operations in business

The importance of operations

The study of operations is concerned with the basic function of enterprise, which is the creation of goods and services. Operations is therefore the core activity of any business and failure to get it 'right' will result in unhappy customers and a production process which is not cost-effective.

Sectors of industry

The consumer lifestyle we enjoy in Scotland is based on an interconnected chain of production which can be shown in three sectors of Industry:

1 **Primary sector:** This sector gathers natural resources which are extracted from the Earth by mining, fishing and forestry, etc.

2 **Secondary sector:** This sector takes production from the Primary Sector and processes it to make finished goods. Any activity such as manufacturing, the construction industry or utility providers (*companies providing water, gas and electricity*) are examples of this sector.

3 **Tertiary sector:** This is also known as the SERVICE SECTOR as their production is intangible (*cannot be seen or physically touched*). This is a growing area in the Scottish economy and includes banking, insurance, tourism and retail.

> **Top Tip**
> Do not confuse the sectors of industry with the sectors of the economy. The sectors of the economy are private and public.

In the provision of goods or services several sectors might be involved. Take for example fish fingers. First the primary sector is involved as fish are caught in the sea. Then a fish processing factory takes the raw materials and makes them into fish fingers. This is a secondary sector industry. Finally, the supermarket sells the fish fingers from its freezers. This is an example of a tertiary sector industry.

Input, process and output

You should be aware of the three main stages in production known as IPO.

INPUT	PROCESS	OUTPUT
This is a list of the raw materials, equipment and labour needed for the creation of the good or service.	This is how the good or service is physically made or provided.	This is the final good or service ready for sale to a consumer or used in another manufacturing process.

The stages are linked. Input leads to process and finally output. Let us take the example of the manufacture of a woollen jumper.

INPUT	PROCESS	OUTPUT
Wool (raw materials) and workers are needed	The garment is knitted	Finally, we have a finished product

Top Tip
IPO equally applies to services. Think of your school – **Inputs** are your teachers, the **Process** is the teaching and the final **Output** is a Credit 1 in Business Management!

Wealth creation

Wealth creation occurs at each stage of the production process. Value is added each time something is done. Wealth creation is concerned with increasing the amount of goods and services available, but it can be measured financially by simply subtracting the cost of the inputs from the value of the finished good or service.

Quick Test

1. Name the sector of industry which extracts raw materials from the Earth.
2. Name the sector of industry which takes the raw materials and makes them into finished goods.
3. What is the other name for the service sector?
4. List three inputs in the production of a car.
5. Describe how wealth creation can be measured.

Answers 1. Primary sector **2.** Secondary sector **3.** Tertiary sector **4.** Labour, steel, rubber, plastic, leather, etc. **5.** Difference between the value of inputs and outputs.

Stock

What is stock?

Stock is the name given to the materials held in a business and can take three different forms:

- **raw materials:** these are used in the production process
- **work-in-progress:** these are partially completed items
- **finished goods:** these are items of stock ready for sale.

The efficient handling of stock is important for any business. Not having sufficient materials will result in missed sales and a poor reputation.

Stock can have a number of hidden costs. There is the cost of storage and security. Most stock will need to be insured. There is also the potential danger that stock might deteriorate, particularly food products, or become unsellable because of changes in demand – this is known as obsolescence.

Many suppliers provide a trade discount for buying in bulk. This helps the supplier as it encourages businesses to buy large quantities, increasing sales and also reducing paperwork and delivery costs. The business also benefits from reduced costs and increased profitability.

Most sales of stock will be on credit. This means that payment is made after the stock has been delivered. A cash discount can be offered by suppliers to encourage businesses to pay promptly; this is often expressed as a percentage discount off the original price.

Reliability and quality are sometimes more important than price in determining a supplier of raw materials. When raw materials are delivered late there is often a knock-on effect on production with the customer being kept waiting or deciding to go elsewhere. High quality inputs may lead to less waste in the production process as well as greater customer satisfaction.

CREDIT

There are two stock control systems that you need to be aware of.

1 **Just-in-time (JIT) stock control:** This method attempts to ensure that there is no stock kept in a business. Raw materials arrive only when they are needed for production and finished goods are dispatched to customers the moment they are completed.

The advantage of JIT is that there will be no stockholding costs such as warehouse rent or security staff wages. The stock is also likely to be fresher, which will result in a higher quality product for the customer.

The disadvantages of JIT are that the business must have a very reliable supplier so that they are able to meet demand as and when it occurs. The administration costs associated with having to keep reordering stock is also likely to be higher.

2 **Economic stock level (ESL) stock control:** This method of stock control identifies three stock levels:

- Maximum stock level – which should never be exceeded, as storage costs or the danger of deterioration is too high.
- Minimum stock level – this level acts as a 'buffer' in case of delays in the arrival of stock. Stock levels should never be allowed to fall below this level.
- Reorder level – this will be set above the minimum stock level and will take account of delivery times from suppliers to ensure that stock arrives just as stock levels reach minimum stock levels.

The advantages of ESL over JIT is that stock should always be available for production, even in cases of unexpected demand, and also, businesses should be able to take advantage of trade discount for buying in bulk.

Top Tip
A possible question at Credit level is to discuss the advantages and disadvantages of JIT.

Top Tip
When asked for the advantages of one system, remember you can often state the disadvantages of another.

Information technology in stock control

When used properly information technology allows for greater speed, interpretation and ease in the flow of information. This can be shown in the handling of stock.

A computerised stock control system such as Electronic Point of Sale (EPOS) can be used to keep track of stock levels, identify those items of stock for which there is a high/low turnover and even be programmed to place orders automatically with suppliers.

Quick Test

1. Name the three forms of stock.
2. Suggest hidden costs of stock.
3. What factors will a manufacturer look for in a supplier?
4. Describe JIT.
5. Name the three stock levels in ESL.

Answers 1. Raw materials, work-in-progress, finished goods. **2.** Storage, security, deterioration, obsolescence. **3.** Trade discount-price, reliability, quality. **4.** Where no stock is held in a business. **5.** Maximum, minimum and reorder levels.

Factors of production

The term factors of production is that given to the resources required to produce goods and services.

Factor of Production	Description
Land	Land is used to describe the gifts of nature used in the production process. These are raw materials which are found on, in or above the Earth. Examples of land are soil, fish, coal and air.
Labour	Labour is the term used to describe any production activity, whether it involves predominately mental or physical effort. Labour may be hired but never owned. Examples of labour are a teacher or a fisherman.
Capital	Capital is the name given to items necessary to produce a good or service. They are of value not for themselves but for what they can do. Examples of capital are machines, vehicles and money.
Enterprise	Enterprise is the most important factor of production as this is the process of bringing together the other factors to produce a good or service. It is carried out through an entrepreneur.

A limitation of one of the factors of production can result in a producer substituting it with one which is more available. For example, a shortage of skilled workers (labour) might result in an entrepreneur investing in machinery (capital).

The interdependence of the factors of production should also be considered. The link between labour and capital can be illustrated where the complex equipment used in hospitals requires very skilled medical staff. The decision to set up a new golf course in Scotland would require a thorough search for the right location; this shows a strong link between enterprise and land.

Top Tip
When trying to remember the **factors of production** try drawing a mind map.

Labour or capital intensive

The amount of capital or labour used in a business can be used to describe that business as either capital intensive or labour intensive.

CAPITAL INTENSIVE is when the amount of Capital used in the businesses is significantly greater than the amount of Labour. Where the production process involves mostly machines it is described as MACHANISED. When the process is carried out purely by machine it is known as AUTOMATED. An example of a Capital Intensive process is the car manufacturer Citroen who manufacture the Csara Picasso.

The main advantages of capital intensive production are that machines do not get tired and they maintain a consistent level of accuracy. However, such machines are often very specialised and lack flexibility. There is also the financial implication of the initial investment and the cost of maintenance.

Labour intensive is where most of the work is carried out by humans. Some types of work lend themselves to this method of production, particularly work in the service sector, such as teaching, nursing or tourism.

Labour intensive will be the preferred method to use where thought or initiative is required. Some call centres are moving away from automated services because customers would rather speak to a 'real' person. There are however a number of costs associated with labour intensive production. Wages are a major factor in most organisations, there is also the hidden cost associated with recruitment and selection such as advertising and training. The amount of time that a human can work is limited and when they get tired or bored the quality of their work can suffer.

Top Tip
When revising many people like to write notes as bullet points. This is great, but remember for your General/Credit exam you will be expected to write in sentences.

Quick Test

1. List the four factors of production.

2. What does capital intensive mean? Give an example of a good which would be produced in this way.

3. What does labour intensive mean? Give an example of a service which would be produced in this way?

Answers 1. Land, labour, capital and enterprise. **2.** Where more capital than labour is used. Examples of goods would be cars, computers, etc. **3.** Where most of the work is carried out by humans. Examples of services would be teaching, nursing, etc.

Production methods

Production can take place in three different ways. It is the role of the entrepreneur to decide on the best method for the good or service being produced.

Job production

This method of production is used when a manufacturer produces a unique or one-off product such as a wedding dress. Here the production process is likely to be labour intensive. As a result, such products are characterised by being very expensive and taking a long time to produce.

Consumers are usually very pleased with items produced through job production as they are manufactured specifically to an individual's requirements, and are normally of a very high standard or quality. The unique nature of the product can command a high price for the manufacturer.

Flow production

This method is also known as mass or line production as it involves the production of identical products in a factory usually on an assembly line. Examples of goods produced in this way are cars and washing machines. Flow production can be seen as the opposite of job production and is likely to be capital intensive with any labour being low skilled.

Top Tip
With Economies of Scale do not confuse unit costs with total costs.

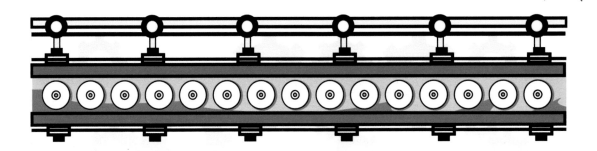

Production in such large amounts can result in economies of scale, which will result in cheaper end products. This is of benefit not only to the manufacturer but also the consumer. Economies of scale are where the unit cost of production falls as a result of the increased number of units produced.

Batch production

This can be seen as a combination of job and flow production A manufacturer will make a large amount of one product, stop, alter the raw materials and machinery, and then make a large amount of another product.

Top Tip
Think of specific examples of goods or services produced in the three different ways.

A Scottish example of batch production is Baxters Ltd who will produce a large amount, or batch, of one type of soup before producing a batch of another type. Batch production tends to be relatively capital intensive.

The main benefit of batch production is that some flexibility can be built into the production process, allowing finished goods to appeal to a variety of customers while still taking advantage of economies of scale. The main disadvantage of batch production is that time is wasted switching from one production batch to another.

Distribution

Distribution involves trying to maximise sales by providing finished products in the right place at the right time.

When trying to decide where to sell products and how to get them to these places, the Operations Department will usually work alongside the Marketing Department.

For many years businesses have supplied their customers via mail order, but increasingly this has been extended to include the Internet and other forms of online shopping such as TV shopping channels like QVC and Price Drop.

Quick Test

1. Which method of production would be best for the manufacture of a unique piece of jewellery?

2. Suggest a production method for the mass production of millions of CD players.

3. A factory makes different types of school uniform. Suggest a suitable type of production process to use.

Answers 1. Job production 2. Flow production 3. Batch production

Quality and Distribution

What is quality?

The quality of output is an issue for every organisation. Reputation and return custom will be determined by the quality of the final good or service. Poor quality production is wasteful, with faulty produce costing Scottish manufacturers millions every year. Poor quality production has even created a new phenomenon where shopping outlets sell 'seconds' at bargain prices.

You are probably familiar with the saying 'rubbish in means rubbish out' To ensure a quality end product it is vital that organisations start with a quality input. This can be fresh raw materials in the manufacturing service or a trained workforce in the service sector.

Top Tip
The customer ultimately defines quality. If they think a product or service is value-for-money they will purchase it.

in

out

Quality is determined by the customer – whether it satisfies their needs and is value for money. An organisation must make sure that the methods of production they use is suitable for the end product. If customers are looking for a mass-produced item such as a toothbrush then the best process will be flow production which will combine quality and standardisation. On the other hand if they are looking for a unique piece of jewellery, the customer will be happy with nothing less than job production were individuality is guaranteed.

Quality can also be pre and post-sales service. A customer might choose to shop in a boutique because of the degree of service they can expect, rather than at a bargain basement. Product guarantees and after-sales service are other important factors in the definition of quality. Buyers are interested in customer service because they usually want to feel that their custom is important and that they matter to the organisation.

There is legislation affecting the quality of the products that a business offers to buyers. These laws must be followed or a business can face court action. Examples of these are the Sale of Goods Act which insists that items offered for sale must be of a suitable standard. The Trade Descriptions Act ensures that exaggerated claims are not made by organisations selling products.

Improving quality

To prevent poor quality a business can use the following activities to ensure or improve quality.

Activity	Description
Quality control	The product is checked at the very end of the production process. Quality control can lead to waste as a faulty product can go through several stages before it is detected.
Quality assurance	Each stage of production is checked to ensure that the product is of a satisfactory standard before moving on to the next stage.
Total quality management (TQM)	There is emphasis on everyone in an organisation to maintain a quality good or service. All staff strive to ensure the end product is of the highest quality. There must be a clear definition of what quality is.
Bench marking	A business compares itself with the best in its field and strives to achieve a similar standard.
Quality circles	Staff from different areas of the business come together to discuss ways in which the organisation can improve. This may involve ways of providing a better service to the public or reducing costs.
Quality standards	Levels of quality are set and recognised outside of an organisation. Examples include the Kite Mark, the Red Lion on eggs and Investors in People (IIP).
Customer feedback	Customers are asked what they think of the business and appropriate action is then taken. Customer questionnaires and suggestion boxes are used by many organisations.

The right place at the right time

Distribution involves trying to maximise sales by providing finished products in the right place and at the right time. When trying to decide where to sell products and how to get them to these places, the operations department will usually work alongside the marketing department.

For many years businesses have supplied their customers via mail order, but increasingly this has been extended to include the Internet and other forms of online shopping such as TV shopping channels like QVC and Price Drop.

Top Tip
E-Commerce is the term used to describe selling via the Internet.

Using computers to generate information

Computers in business

Computers have transformed businesses, especially small businesses. The use of personal computers (PCs) has meant that small to very large businesses now have access to a wide range of software applications which helps them to run their business.

The main use of software applications is to generate information to help the business make decisions. The information may come from a word processor, spreadsheet, database or other piece of software but the end result is the same – the information obtained helps to run the business.

Software packages

Software package	Description and business use
Word processing	A word processing program allows the user to create, edit and save documents. Documents produced include letters, memos, notices, forms, newsletters, etc. Any written document can be saved and amended before printing. Microsoft Word is one example.
Spreadsheet	A spreadsheet program is used for numerical calculations. Spreadsheets have made the jobs of accountants much easier by allowing formulas to be used to calculate and re-calculate budgets, trading and profit and loss accounts and balance sheets. All financial calculations can be done on a spreadsheet saving hours of work. Microsoft Excel is one example
Database	A database program allows the user to create, store, edit and update records. The database allows reports to be produced quickly and easily therefore allowing managers to make quick decisions. Microsoft Access is one example.
Desk top publishing (DTP)	This type of software is used to produce leaflets, newsletters and magazines. It allows any user to produce professional documents. The documents are usually printed on high quality laser printers and often in colour. 888 is one example.

Software package	Description and business use
Integrated software package 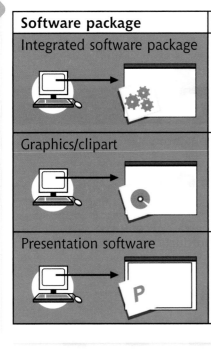	An integrated software package has word processing, database, spreadsheet, and graphics all integrated. The advantage is that all the programs are easily accessible and files can be transferred easily. Clarisworks is one example.
Graphics/clipart	Graphics programs allow graphs and diagrams to be produced by the computer. Spreadsheet programs have the facility to draw graphs. Clipart can be inserted from a CD-ROM. Free diagrams available on the Internet, e.g. Google images.
Presentation software	Presentation software allows the user to create slideshows in order to display information. Slides can contain text, graphs, photographs, video clips, etc. Microsoft Powerpoint is an example.

Using computers to generate information and make decisions

In business computers are used to provide information in order to make decisions. Modern ICT equipment and software means that there is far more information available than ever before in order to make these decisions. Also the information is available much quicker than before. Reports, documents, diagrams, plans, etc. can be printed out and updated on a daily basis. Files can be emailed around the world, and networks allow data to be shared. A business executive has information at the touch of a few keys from the world wide web.

Top Tip

A business executive uses ICT as a tool for decision making. It is the information obtained from the computer that is important.

Quick Test

Describe the following software packages and give one business use for each of them.

1. Word processor
2. Database
3. Presentation software
4. Email

Answers 1. Allows the user to create, edit and save documents. Variety of fonts, styles, tables and graphics can be used. Business uses are – preparing letters, memos, advertisements etc. **2.** Allows the user to create, store, edit and update records. Records can be kept of suppliers, customers etc. Business uses are – customer records, stock records. **3.** Allows the user to create slides, pages to be used to display information normally using a data projector. Slides can contain graphics, animation etc. Business uses – presentations to employees on health and safety, during interviews applicants might be asked to make a presentation.

How ICT is used in business

How ICT is used in marketing

- **Spreadsheet:** Used for analysing sales figures and producing graphs from figures.
- **Database:** Customer information held, reports produced for market segments, information on competitors and their products held.
- **DTP/graphics:** Used to produce advertisements, graphs and charts of sales figures, pictures and posters for customers, leaflets to advertise products, etc.
- **Internet:** Websites can be set up to advertise products and allow customers to buy on-line.

Important decisions for marketing managers to make from ICT information include:

- What area or sales person has been the most successful?
- What group (market segment) is going to be targeted with a new product?
- What competitors are selling at a lower price than us and do we need to change our prices?

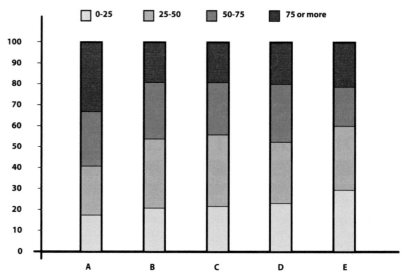

How ICT is used in finance

- **Spreadsheet:** Invoices can be set up to record all customer purchases. The spreadsheet performs all calculations and produces invoices. Records all cheques paid and payments received. Calculations are performed quickly and accurately. Bring together financial information for all aspects of the business and produces final accounts. Used for budgets and cash flow. This allows the business to forecast into the future and change figures without having to re-calculate.

Important decisions for finance managers to make from ICT information include:

- Which customers still have bills to be paid and how much?
- How much cash do we have in the bank?
- What was the profit last year compared to this year?
- What is the total of our bills or expenses and where do we need to cut down?

Top Tip
Make sure you know what a cash budget is and what it is used for.

How ICT is used in human resources

- **Word processing:** Job applications, interview letters, job descriptions, etc.
- **Database:** Storing employee information, such as name, address, etc. as well as appraisal reports, absence, extra qualifications, training courses, grade of employee. Records also held on previous applicants for posts and searches can be done to find suitable candidates for a vacancy.
- **Spreadsheet:** Analysis of salaries/wages throughout the organisation.

Important decisions for human resources managers to make from ICT information include:

- How many employees do we have on Grade 2?
- How many employees were absent for more than three weeks last year?
- How many candidates applied for each of our vacancies last month?
- What is the total salary paid to employees in the administration section?

How ICT is used in operations

- **Database:** Records stock levels. Stock lists can be updated quickly and easily and stock re-ordered when necessary.
- **Specialist software:** Computer aided design and manufacturing used for design and manufacture of products. Robots and machines used for production lines and quality control.

Important decisions for operations managers to make from ICT information include:

- How many items of stock do we have?
- What is the total value of stock?
- What stock has been re-ordered today?
- What products have failed the quality control test and why?

Top Tip

ICT is used in different ways in different functional areas. You should be able to describe the different uses – e.g. Don't always describe the use of a word processor.

Quick Test

1. Give two ways in which ICT could be used in marketing.
2. Give two ways in which ICT could be used in finance.
3. Identify three important decisions that human resources managers might make using ICT.

Using ICT to communicate

Features of Internet websites

Many businesses have acknowledged the power of an Internet website for additional advertising and on-line selling. This is often known as e-commerce or e-business.

Internet websites are all different; they use different colours, fonts, layouts, etc. Website designers put a lot of thought, time and effort into developing business websites. The main aim of the designer is that the website should be easy to access and easy to use.

Some of the design features that are included in popular websites are as follows:

- colourful text which is easy to read
- graphics and photographs to catch attention
- hyperlinks to link to other websites of interest
- video clips and audio recordings
- easy navigation (it is easy to follow the website)
- good layout which is not confusing
- consistency of font and layout across all pages of the website.

Information which is usually included on a business website includes:

- business contact details, such as the name and address of the business
- details of products and services, and an on-line shop with photographs and prices
- secure payment section for customers to pay on-line (e-commerce)
- business information, such as when the business was set up, its aims and objectives
- recruitment section giving job vacancies
- frequently asked questions (FAQs) for help to customers.

Top Tip
You need to know the difference between the features of a website and the information contained on a website.

Main methods of ICT communication

ICT method of communication	Description and business use
Internet	The Internet is a world-wide network of computers. It is an electronic source of information containing millions of pages from many different sources. Any user can set up their own website in order to communicate with customers.

ICT method of communication	Description and business use
Email	Email is short for electronic mail. Connecting to the Internet allows you to use email to communicate with computers all over the world. Short messages are usually sent but reports and photographs can be attached to them. Email is fast and inexpensive.
Voicemail	Voicemail is the modern version of an answering machine. Electronic switchboards now allow callers to be put through to the extension of the person they are trying to call to leave a message.
Answering machine	Answering machines allow messages to be left when there is no-one to answer the phone. This way the business can still receive important calls from customers and suppliers. All messages have to be transcribed and forwarded to the correct person.
Mobile telephone	Mobile phones and text messages have transformed the way that individuals and businesses keep in touch. Mobiles allows individuals to be contacted most of the time. Many businesses now send text messages to their customers as a means of advertising.
Pager	A pager is used to contact someone who is perhaps not near a telephone or where a mobile phone does not work. It sends a simple message telling the individual to contact a number. Often used on building sites or in hospitals.
Telephone System	Business telephone systems are linked to computer networks and voicemail. The telephone is as much a part of ICT now as a PC. Telephones are used daily in business for immediate contact.
Computer network	Computer networks can be large or small. They can be based within one room, one building or across the country. They allow the whole business to share data and additional equipment such as printers. Networks allow a business to have their own intranet.

Top Tip
In the examination you should always use the phrase 'Internet website' and not just Internet. You should give as much information as possible about where you would find information on the Internet. However you do not need to know specific website addresses.

Quick Test

Describe the following methods of ICT communication and give one business use for each of them:

1. The Internet
2. Email
3. A computer network

The benefits and problems of ICT communication

Advantages and disadvantages of using ICT to communicate

Method of ICT	Advantages	Disadvantages
Internet	Easily accessible; good advertising for business	Website can crash causing frustration for customers; hackers can break into websites
Email	Quick and easy to send; not very expensive compared to ordinary post	Not everyone has email; not useful for confidential information; not everyone checks email every day
Voicemail	Good for receiving messages when business is closed; can get straight through to the person you want to leave a message for	Sometimes messages are not very clear; some customers do not like leaving messages
Answering machine	Good for receiving messages when the business is closed; cheap to buy and easy to install	Sometimes messages are not very clear
Mobile telephone	Easy to reach people when out of the office; text messages are quick and easy to understand	Signal can sometimes be poor; text messages can be misunderstood; can be expensive to run
Pager	Quick and easy to use; portable and inexpensive, good when mobile phone signals are poor	Can only alert person to contact a telephone or give a very short message
Telephone system	Quick and easy to use; almost everyone has a telephone, easily understood	Difficult for time barriers; sometimes lines can be disrupted
Computer network	Easy to share information; can share programs; easy to share equipment; can have a business Intranet	If network crashes no-one can work; data can be corrupted if viruses occur; hackers can break into the network and cause damage

Choosing the most appropriate method of ICT

All of the above methods of communication are available to businesses and individuals. However, not all businesses have intranets or computer networks. The ICT methods used depend on a number of different factors and situations.

In order to communicate effectively using ICT the following factors have to be taken into account:

- What equipment does the business have?
- What are the skills of the staff?
- How much will it cost to communicate?
- Is the message very long or very short?
- Is the message confidential?
- Is the information to be communicated complicated?
- Are there any time barriers involved?
- Is the message urgent?

Problems of using ICT to communicate

Depending on the method chosen and the skills and experience of the users, there are many different problems which can occur when communicating with ICT. These include:

- machines and equipment can break down
- mobile phone signals may be weak
- emails are not checked regularly
- computer networks can crash
- confidential emails can be intercepted
- staff need training
- websites can crash
- pagers, mobile phones and laptops can run out of battery power
- text messages may not be understood if they contain too much slang.

Justifying the use of ICT in different contexts

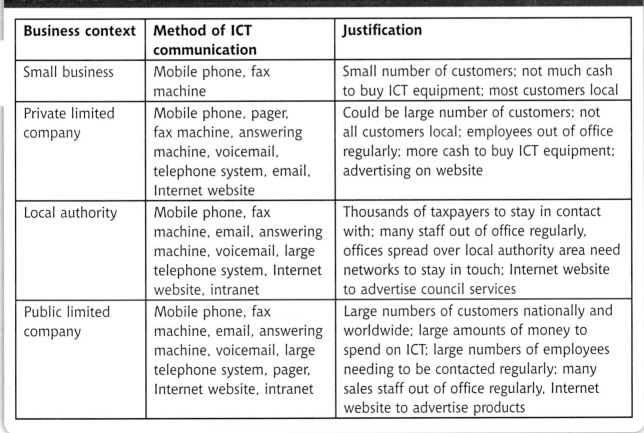

Business context	Method of ICT communication	Justification
Small business	Mobile phone, fax machine	Small number of customers; not much cash to buy ICT equipment; most customers local
Private limited company	Mobile phone, pager, fax machine, answering machine, voicemail, telephone system, email, Internet website	Could be large number of customers; not all customers local; employees out of office regularly; more cash to buy ICT equipment; advertising on website
Local authority	Mobile phone, fax machine, email, answering machine, voicemail, large telephone system, Internet website, intranet	Thousands of taxpayers to stay in contact with; many staff out of office regularly, offices spread over local authority area need networks to stay in touch; Internet website to advertise council services
Public limited company	Mobile phone, fax machine, email, answering machine, voicemail, large telephone system, pager, Internet website, intranet	Large numbers of customers nationally and worldwide; large amounts of money to spend on ICT; large numbers of employees needing to be contacted regularly; many sales staff out of office regularly, Internet website to advertise products

Recruitment and selection

Definitions

The human resources department of a business is responsible for choosing the right people to fit any vacancies in the business. Human resources play a very important role in making sure that the business has good quality workers with the proper skills and qualifications. Recruitment means getting candidates to apply for jobs in the first place. Selection means choosing the right person for the job once you have considered all the applications.

The recruitment and selection process follows a number of steps which are common to many businesses.

Top Tip
Make sure you understand the difference between recruitment and selection.

Internal recruitment

Internal recruitment is when a job vacancy is filled from within the existing staff. There are different ways to do this. The job may be advertised internally and all candidates who want to apply can do so. The certainty is that an internal candidate will get the job.

The job may also be filled by upgrading an employee, perhaps after an interview. There may also be recommendations from supervisors or managers, or an employee may be approached to fill the new vacancy.

When the job is filled internally employees can often feel that someone has been 'favoured' and feel resentment. On the other hand they can feel motivated that they have a better chance as there is no candidate from outside. Although the business knows the internal candidate well and what they are capable of doing, it misses out on the opportunity to bring in fresh 'blood' and new ideas.

External recruitment

External recruitment is when a vacancy is filled from open competition and advertisement. Existing employees will be allowed to apply, but applications are also invited from outside. The job may be advertised locally, nationally or internationally.

Jobs can be advertised in newspapers, magazines, on Internet websites, in job centres, etc. Wherever the job is advertised it will attract applications and candidates will go through the recruitment process.

Alternatively the business may ask a recruitment agency to find them a suitable candidate. The agency will take responsibility for advertising the job right through to interviewing the candidates. This is useful if the business is very small and does not have the expertise for recruiting. Large businesses also use agencies as it is less time consuming for them.

External recruitment brings in new people who will have fresh ideas and can be a motivating factor for existing employees. However, the opposite can also be the case. Employees may not like the changes and resent the new employee. Existing employees may also feel resentful that they didn't get the job.

Top Tip

Make sure you can outline the advantages and disadvantages of both internal and external recruitment.

Quick Test

1. What is internal recruitment?
2. What is external recruitment?
3. Give one advantage and one disadvantage of internal recruitment.
4. Give one advantage and one disadvantage of external recruitment.

1. Internal recruitment is when a job vacancy is filled from within the existing staff. 2. External recruitment is when a vacancy is filled from open competition and advertisement. Existing employees will be allowed to apply but applications are invited from outside. 3. Adv – Increased motivation of employees Disadv – Some employees may be resentful of person who gets the job. 4. Adv – Fresh ideas can be brought into the business. Disadv – Existing employees may not like changes.

Choosing the right person for the job

The job analysis

When a business thinks it may have a vacancy they will prepare a job analysis in the first instance. This will outline the need for the job and confirm such details as what the job is and where it will be. After this a job advertisement will be prepared and placed in the appropriate place.

Job advertisements

Job advertisements can appear in:

- government job centres;
- recruitment agencies;
- newspapers;
- radio/television;
- the internet
- shop windows.

The job advertisement has to be very clear and should include details such as:

- job title
- salary
- hours of work
- duties involved
- location
- how to apply (whether to complete an application form or send in a CV).

Application forms

Application forms vary in length and quality. If the business has prepared an application form they will send this out to any applicants who contact the business and ask for one. An application form asks for the same information from each candidate, such as name, address, date of birth, qualifications, experience, references, etc. The advantage to the business of receiving application forms is that the information is very similar from each candidate and it makes it easier to process.

On-line applications are becoming more and more popular. Applicants complete an application form on the website of the business. This is very quick for the business to receive and easy for the applicant. The only one drawback for the business is that they cannot be sure that it was completed by the applicant.

CVs

CV is short for curriculum vitae. This is a document which is prepared by the applicant to his or her own design. It includes all relevant personal details such as name, address, date of birth, qualifications, experience, etc. A CV allows a candidate to give much more personal detail about themselves than an application form.

Job description

A job description is usually prepared after the job analysis has been completed and the job advertisement is prepared and ready to be placed. The job description gives all the essential details about the job and is sent to each applicant. The job description will include:

- job title
- duties and responsibilities
- location
- salary
- working conditions and holidays
- any benefits.

An example is shown right:

The job description has to give a very clear picture of what the job entails so that there will be no misunderstandings once the right candidate has been chosen.

Administration Manager
Glasgow
Job description
Duties
Manage a busy export office
Support the Director
Prepare documents in Microsoft Office.
Supervise junior staff
Organise holiday rotas
Salary £23,000

Person specification

A person specification is also prepared after the job analysis has been done. This outlines details of the type of person the business is looking for to do the job. The person specification will include essential and desirable attributes. Essential means the applicant must have them. Desirable means it would be better if they have them. A simple person specification is shown right.

Administration Manager	
Person specification	
Essential attributes	*Desirable attributes*
ICT skills	Driving licence
Management skills	Ability to speak
Communication skills	French
HND qualification or similar	

The business recruiting the new employee will carefully match the person specification with all the application forms and CVs they receive to see who they wish to interview for the post.

Top Tip
A job description is about the job. A person specification is about the person the business is looking for.

Quick Test

1. Explain the difference between a job description and a person specification.
2. Suggest three places where a job advertisement can be placed.
3. What are the advantages and disadvantages of on-line applications?
4. What is the difference between an application form and a CV?

1. Job description outlines details of the job eg salary, duties, whereas person specification outlines details about the person required eg qualities and skills. 2. Job Centres, Recruitment Agencies, Newspapers, TV, Radio, Internet Websites 3. Adv – Easy for applicant to complete and can be sent immediately it is finished Standard form so employers can get exact information they want Disadv – Employers do not know if applicant has completed form themselves May not let applicant tell all about themselves 4. Application forms designed by business and each form has identical information. CV completed by individual and no 2 CVs are likely to be the same. CV allows more personal information to be included.

The selection process

Shortlisting candidates

Once all the applications have been received they are read by the human resources department. They will carefully select those applicants that they think have the necessary skills, qualifications and experience to do the job. They will compare the applications received with the person specification and match up good candidates.

They will prepare a shortlist of candidates who will be invited to the selection procedures. The most common form of selection procedure is an interview but there are others.

The interview

The business has to prepare for the interview process in order to make it fair and equal for all the candidates.

Before the interview they will decide on an interview panel. They will also decide where and when the interviews will take place. Most importantly they will prepare suitable interview questions.

All candidates will be invited to the interview in writing.

During the interview the panel will make notes on what each candidate is saying. At the end of all interviews the panel will carefully compare all the answers and begin to decide who the best candidate is.

In order to assist with the selection, the panel will also consider references for the applicants. References or referees provide a report on the applicant to back up their application.

Once the final decision has been made the successful candidate will be informed and they will arrange to start work. All the unsuccessful candidates will be informed in writing.

Top Tip
An interview is one of the most important methods of selection but it is not the only method used in business.

Other selection methods

Some businesses will use other methods to select the best candidate. They may do this instead of or as well as an interview.

- Presentation: Candidates may be asked to make a presentation to the panel. This could involve using a flip chart, overhead projector or a computer and data projector. The topic for the presentation would usually be given to the candidates in advance.

- Role-play: Candidates may be asked to take part in a scenario which show how they react in different situations, such as dealing with a difficult customer. The role-play is designed to show the strengths, weaknesses and personality of the candidates.

- Group discussion or group interview: Candidates may be asked to take part in a discussion with all the other shortlisted candidates for the job. This is to try and see who emerges as natural leaders and what type of interpersonal skills the candidates have.

- Personality tests/ability tests: These are usually done along with some other form of selection process. The idea behind tests is simply to find out knowledge, ability and personality of the candidates. Many of these tests are now done on-line.

Top Tip
You should be able to describe at least two methods of selection in addition to interviews.

Quick Test

1. Describe what happens during the interview process.

2. Name and describe two other methods of selecting candidates.

Answers 1. Interview panel ask all applicants same questions. Panel makes notes of what each candidate is saying. Answers are compared at the end and they decide who was best overall. **2.** Presentation – applicants make a presentation to panel – could be flip chart, or powerpoint. Role play – applicants take part in an 'acted out' scenario to see how they react. Group discussion or interview – applicants are all put together to see whether leaders emerge from the discussion. Personality tests/ability tests – can be done on-line. Trying to assess personality and knowledge eg numeracy.

Working in business today

Working hours are very different to what they were 20 years ago. There are different patterns of working and different types of worker. The days of 9–5 for everyone have gone.

Types of workers

- **Professional workers** are sometimes known as white collar workers. They usually have qualifications such as university degrees or diplomas. Professional workers include teachers, doctors, lawyers, accountants and engineers.
- **Skilled workers** have specialist qualifications in their field. They will have been trained at college or their place of work and will have certificates, e.g. plumbers, electricians and hairdressers. Their training has usually been specifically for the particular job.
- **Semiskilled workers** do not have specialist qualifications but will have been trained in their job or may have acquired skills from a number of different jobs throughout their working life. Semiskilled workers include shop keepers, shop assistants and call centre operators.
- **Unskilled or manual workers** have very few formal qualifications. They are sometimes known as blue collar workers. They will be employed as labourers, road sweepers, cleaners and car park attendants. All jobs require a basic level of skill for that particular job.

Contract of employment

Employees receive a written contract of employment within two months of starting work. This contract should outline the conditions of the job and will contain many of the details from the job description. The contract of employment will contain the following information:

- name of employer
- name of employee
- date of staring work
- job title
- duties of the job
- salary or pay
- hours of work
- holidays
- place of work

Types of training

Training is now a standard part of a job. Almost all businesses and organisations offer their employees some form of training. The purpose of training is to improve the knowledge, skills, qualifications and motivation of employees. There are different forms of training.

- **Induction training** is offered to new employees and usually concentrates on the business and its environment, rather than on the employee's specific job. Induction training may include:
  - Health and Safety issues
  - arrangements for signing in and out
  - social arrangements, such as where to have coffee
  - business or company policies
  - arrangements for holidays
  - sickness arrangements.

Induction training only lasts a short time and will then be followed up by training related to the specific job of the employee.

- **On-the-job-training** is offered to all employees. It is part of the ongoing development of employees to train them to improve their knowledge, skills and performance at work. It is done in the workplace by supervisors, managers or other work colleagues. Training can involve demonstrations, role play, practical exercises, videos, computer assisted learning, etc.

Advantages:

- Training is usually geared specifically towards the job.
- It takes place at work so no time is wasted travelling elsewhere.
- Employees all know one another so they feel comfortable.

Disadvantages:

- Time is lost on 'real work'.
- Some employees may feel uncomfortable learning with each other.

- **Off-the-job-training** is done away from the work place. This usually involves attending a college or training centre and can result in extra qualifications or certificates. The training is usually done by an expert in the field.

Advantages:

- Employees are trained by experts so quality of training is high.
- Employees can be motivated by receiving additional qualifications.
- Employees are away from the workplace so can concentrate on the training.

Disadvantages:

- Employees are away from the workplace so time is lost from the job.
- It is expensive to pay the trainers as well as give employees time off work.

Top Tip
You should be able to distinguish clearly between on-the-job, off-the-job and induction training.

Quick Test

1. Identify three things which would be contained in a contract of employment.
2. Explain the term 'on-the-job training'.
3. Explain the term 'off-the-job training'.
4. Who is induction training aimed at?
5. Identify three things which would be included in induction training.

Staff appraisals

The role of appraisals

An appraisal is a method of making sure that employees are working to the best of their ability and achieving the business aims. Appraisals aim to measure or evaluate the performance of staff in order to assess their strengths and weaknesses. They may result in pay rises, promotion or additional training courses. They can be both formal and informal.

Formal appraisals

A formal appraisal is usually carried out by a line manager and involves an interview and assessment of performance. The employee should know in advance that the appraisal interview is going to take place and be given the chance to prepare for it. The appraisal interview will be set against agreed targets and is based on evidence of work rate, output and performance. Formal appraisals may result in:

- promotion
- a pay rise
- attendance at training courses
- setting targets for performance
- improved communication
- increased motivation.

Top Tip
An appraisal must have an outcome, ie the employee must know how to improve after being appraised.

During the appraisal interview the employee and line manager will agree a course of action for the coming year. As a result of this interview the employee will have new targets. These targets have to meet the 'SMART' test. Targets have to be:

- specific – they have to be for that particular employee
- measurable – they must be capable of being measured in some way, e.g. increase output by 10 per cent
- agreed – both the employee and the line manager have to agree
- realistic – the targets have to be achievable, i.e. not too difficult or too easy
- timed – there should be a time by which the targets should be achieved, e.g. 2 months.

Advantages of formal appraisals	Disadvantages of formal appraisals
The format is agreed in advance – there are no surprises for the employee	Employee may not get on with their line manager and feel the process is unfair
They can result in pay rises or promotion for employees who are working hard	Employees may feel criticised and insecure in their jobs
Employees receive positive feedback and therefore feel more motivated	Motivation can decrease if employees feel worried or threatened by appraisals
Strengths are identified and good workers rewarded	Workload can increase if too many targets are set during the interview

Top Tip
Remember the SMART test for target setting.

Informal appraisals

Informal appraisals do not have a structure and in many cases the employee may not even know they are being appraised. Informal appraisals may be based on observation of employees and 'feelings' or impressions of how they are getting on in their job. They usually arise naturally with employees and management working closely together on a daily basis. There is not usually an agreed set of guidelines or targets so the appraisal cannot usually be used for pay rises, promotion, etc.

Advantages of informal appraisals	Disadvantages of informal appraisals
Employees are relaxed in their work	Employees may not know they are being appraised
Line managers can see clearly the work that is being done	No set criteria are used therefore it may not always be fair to all employees
Good relationships can be formed	Not useful for pay rises, promotion, etc. as no evidence produced from the appraisal
Motivation can be increased if employees are not threatened by the process of appraisal	Employees may feel that some are favoured more than others.

Quick Test

1. Explain the term 'formal appraisal'.

2. Identify two advantages and two disadvantages of formal appraisals.

3. Explain the term 'informal appraisal'.

4. Identify two advantages and two disadvantages of informal appraisals.

Interrelationships between employees and employers

In order for businesses to be successful and employees to be happy in their work there has to be a good working relationship between the employees and their employers. This is not always possible, however, because both groups can want different things.

Trade unions

A trade union is an organisation that employees can join in order to help them negotiate better pay and conditions. A trade union will advise union members, will step in and help to resolve disputes with employers, and bargain on behalf of its members. It may also offer additional benefits such as financial services and legal advice.

There are lots of different trade unions. Some are specialised and members must belong to a particular profession, others are more general and cover a range of different jobs. In Scotland the EIS union represents teachers whereas UNISON represents public sector workers such as janitors, cleaners, nurses, etc.

Disputes

When a trade union has to negotiate with employers, the process is called collective bargaining. The Trade Union represents hundreds of employees therefore it has a strong bargaining position. The aim is to come to an agreement which both sides can implement. Disputes may arise over rates of pay, working conditions, introduction of new machinery, etc.

Top Tip
Trade unions aim to help employees and employers to work out areas of difficulty and to make sure that working relationships are positive.

Industrial action

When no agreement can be reached between the employer and trade union industrial action can occur. There are different methods of industrial action; and some more damaging than others. All forms of industrial action penalise the business, but employees can suffer too. Profits will be lost and relationships can suffer. Therefore businesses will try to avoid any such action.

The table below shows the different methods of industrial action and the effects on the employer.

Method of industrial action	Advantage to employer	Disadvantage to employer
Strike – employees refuse to go to work and do not get paid	Save wage costs during strike	Production and output lost therefore profits down; business reputation is damaged
Overtime ban – employees refuse to work overtime and lose payment	Save wage costs of overtime; production still takes place	Some orders cannot be met therefore customers not happy
Sit-in – employees occupy the premises but refuse to work; employees lose pay	Save wage costs if employees are not working	Production and output do not take place; bad publicity
Work to rule – employees only do exactly what their contract states; goodwill is lost and some overtime payments may be lost	Production still takes place	Output will fall therefore some orders cannot be met; profits will decrease

No matter what method of action the employee takes they will lose their wage or salary for the time that they are not working. It is in their interest therefore to keep industrial action to a minimum.

There can be positive benefits from industrial action, such as new procedures being introduced. Employees may feel they have been listened to and will work harder.

Top Tip
Remember that industrial action means more than just a strike. Very often a strike is a last resort if no other solutions can be found.

Quick Test

1. Describe the role and purpose of a trade union.
2. Identify two types of industrial action and describe the effect they can have on a business.

Legislation affecting businesses

The role of ACAS

ACAS is the Advisory, Conciliation and Arbitration Service. It provides help to businesses who cannot solve their own disputes, for example, if negotiation has already taken place and has broken down or if there has been lengthy industrial action with no positive outcome.

ACAS will advise employees and employers on a range of matters relating to employment, health and safety, contracts, legislation, etc.

Conciliation is the process whereby the employers and employees are brought together to find solutions to their problems. ACAS does not offer the solutions it simply provides the basis for both sides to talk.

Arbitration takes place when ACAS appoints an independent arbitrator to make a ruling on a dispute. Both sides have to agree whether the result will be binding or not.

Legislation

There are numerous laws relating to the workplace which cover employment, working conditions, health and safety, rights and equality.

Top Tip
You are not expected to know these laws in detail but you are expected to have a basic understanding of what the law is trying to do.

- **Equal Pay Act 1970:** This dates from the time when men were paid more than women for most jobs. This was mainly because women did not make up as big a percentage of the workforce as they do now. The law states that men and women must be given equal pay for equal work or work of equal value.

- **Health and Safety at Work Act 1974:** This outlines the responsibilities of employers and employees in relation to health and safety at work. Employers have a duty to:
  - -provide and maintain safety equipment and safe systems of work
  - -ensure materials used are properly stored, handled, used and transported
  - -provide information, training, instruction and supervision
  - -provide a safe place of employment
  - -have health and safety representatives.

- **Sex Discrimination Act 1975 and 1985:** This does not allow either men or women to be discriminated against in the workplace. A job cannot be kept for either a man or a woman, it must be open to both sexes. Employers will have to show that they treat both men and women equally.

- **Race Relations Act 1976:** This does not allow any man or woman to be discriminated against because of their ethnic origin or colour of their skin. Again, employers will have to show that they treat all ethnic candidates equally.
- **Employment Act 2002:** This is a very wide-ranging act covering the rights of a variety of workers, including:
  - disputes in the workplace
  - maternity and adoption leave and pay
  - paternity leave and pay
  - equal pay claims
  - flexible working
  - young workers rights.
- **Minimum Wage Act 2006:** This stipulates the minimum wage that must be paid to employees. The rate must be paid to all employees over school-leaving age. There is no set rate for employees under this age. The rate is set by the government and will increase over time. The act is intended to help people in low paid jobs to earn a decent wage.
- **Disability Discrimination Act 1995:** This aims to end the discrimination that many disabled people face in many areas of employment. Businesses have to make provision for people with a disability by adapting their premises to allow wheelchair access, and not discriminating against disabled people in interviews.

The impact of all this legislation on a business is that they have to comply with the laws. This may involve additional costs for them and therefore a potential drop in profits.

Quick Test

1. Name three laws which affect recruitment in the workplace.
2. For each of the three laws you have named describe how they affect the business.

Answers 1. Equal Pay Act 1970, Health and Safety at work Act 1974, Sex Discrimination Act 1975 and 1985, Race Relations Act 1976, Employment Act 2002, Minimum Wage Act 2006, Disability Discrimination Act 1995. (choose 3) **2.** Equal Pay Act 1970 – men and women must be given equal pay for equal work of equal value – business has to ensure this happens. Health and Safety at work Act 1974 – affects recruitment in that applicants must be sure that they will be given health and safety training. Sex Discrimination Act 1975 and 1985 – Men or women cannot be discriminated against in the workplace. Jobs must be open to both. Race Relations Act 1976 – Men or women cannot be discriminated against because of the colour of their skin or ethnic origin. Employment Act 2002 – employers have to provide a range of rights to employees including adoption leave, maternity leave etc. Minimum Wage Act 2006 – A fixed sum must be paid to all employees over school leaving age. This is set by the government. Disability Discrimination Act 1995 – Businesses have to make provision for people with a disability to work in their premises by installing lifts, ramps etc.

Changing patterns of employment

The types of businesses in the UK have changed over the past 30 years. The UK has a history of manufacturing industries such as steel, shipping, mining, car production, etc. However, many of these traditional manufacturing industries have declined due to changes in consumer demand and competition from abroad.

There has been a subsequent growth in the service or tertiary sector in the UK economy. There are now more and more businesses offering tourism, retailing, banking, finance, entertainment and other services. Working hours and patterns have changed.

Flexible working practices

While many businesses do still work traditional 9–5 hours, many more do not. Working hours can vary from job to job and from business to business

- **Full-time:** Employees work an agreed number of hours, usually 35–45 hours per week. The hours can be spread over the whole week, or limited to Monday to Friday.
- **Part-time:** Employees work an agreed number of hours from 1 up to around 30 hours per week. The hours can be spread over the whole week or limited to Monday to Friday.
- **Permanent:** Permanent employees expect to stay in their job for a while. They have a contract which states that they work for the business on a permanent basis.
- **Temporary:** Employees do not expect to stay in their job forever. They know that their contract will stop after an agreed time. It could be days, months or even years, but the conditions are agreed at the beginning of the contract.
- **Contract:** Employees are taken on to complete a specific contract or 'job'. The contract could last weeks, months or years, but whenever the contract is finished the employee expects to leave the business.
- **Flexitime:** Employees work an agreed number of hours per week, but they can vary their starting and finishing times. Most employees have a 'core' time when they have to be at work and this is usually 10 am–4 pm. Employees can work extra hours and bank these for time off.

- **Job sharing:** This is a job which is done by more than one person, usually two. The employees share the job on an equal basis, or any other combination that they agree. This is very attractive to employees with family responsibilities.

- **Casual working:** Employees work on the basis that they will only be needed some of the time, but they cannot always be told in advance. This gives no job security and is not usually suitable for people who are looking for a permanent job. This type of work is common in tourism, fruit-picking or jobs associated with Christmas.

- **Homeworking:** Many businesses now allow employees to work at home. Homeworking involves many different types of jobs from sewing, arts and crafts, editing, word processing, etc. Employees who work at home are usually provided with the equipment they need in order to do so.

- **Teleworking:** This also involves working at home but with the use of ICT. A teleworker will spend most of their working day using ICT. They will need a PC, printer, modem, email software and office applications software such as Microsoft Office. Video-conferencing allows employees to use a screen and PC to hold a meeting with other colleagues.

Top Tip
Make sure you know the ICT equipment needed by a teleworker and how they use this equipment to stay in touch with their employer.

Quick Test

1. Explain the following working practices:
   - job-sharing
   - flexi-time
   - homeworking
   - teleworking.

2. Identify one advantage and one disadvantage to the employee of teleworking.

3. Identify one advantage and one disadvantage to the employer of teleworking.

Answers 1. Job-sharing – a job done by more than one person (usually 2). Job is shared on an agreed basis as is pay. Flexi-time – employees work an agreed number of hours but can vary their starting and finishing times. Homeworking - Employees who work from home doing a variety of jobs but not always using ICT eg sewing, proof-reading. Teleworking – employees who work from home but use ICT most of their working day eg PC, fax, video-conferencing etc. **2.** Adv – Can save time and money on travelling Disadv – Lack of contact with colleagues can lead to isolation. **3.** Adv – less office space is needed therefore saving costs Disadv – harder to keep track of what employees are doing.

Planning and controlling finance

Financial planning

All businesses, whether large or small, have to plan and control their finances. In a large business or organisation there will be a specialist section to deal with this called the finance department. In a smaller business or organisation which does not have a finance department some outside help may be required, such as an accountant.

Businesses or organisations have to plan what they are going to spend their money on, i.e. what bills they will have to pay (expenses). They also try to estimate what their income is going to be, i.e. how much they are going to sell and at what price (sales revenue).

Businesses aim to make a profit; this means they will have more sales revenue than expenses.

There are strategies that can be used in order to help plan and control finance and therefore reduce the risk of the business failing.

Fixed costs

Fixed costs are the bills or expenses that the business has to pay that do not change according to output. Fixed costs always have to be paid. If sales are good then fixed costs can easily be covered. If sales are poor there is less sales revenue to cover the fixed costs and therefore less profit.

Examples of fixed costs are: rent of factory, manager's salary, council tax, rates.

Top Tip
Fixed costs do not change as output changes. They always have to be paid. Examples of fixed costs are: rent of factory, manager's salary, council tax, rates.

Variable costs

Variable costs are the bills and expenses that the business has to pay that change according to output. The more a business produces the more the variable costs are going to be. Variable costs are the cost of materials for the product, the cost of labour, etc.

Examples of variable costs are: raw materials, wages, electricity, gas.

Top Tip
Variable costs rise or fall as according to output.

Total costs

The total costs of production are found when the business adds together fixed and variable costs. Once all costs have been calculated the business can then start to work out profits or losses.

Top Tip
Total costs = fixed costs + variable costs

Break even point

The break even point is the point at which total sales revenue and total costs are equal. At this point the business is not making either a profit or a loss. Any sales above the break even point mean the business will make a profit. This can be seen clearly in the graph below

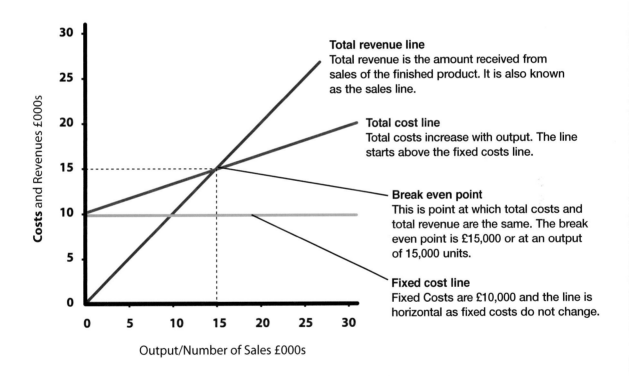

Total revenue line
Total revenue is the amount received from sales of the finished product. It is also known as the sales line.

Total cost line
Total costs increase with output. The line starts above the fixed costs line.

Break even point
This is point at which total costs and total revenue are the same. The break even point is £15,000 or at an output of 15,000 units.

Fixed cost line
Fixed Costs are £10,000 and the line is horizontal as fixed costs do not change.

Quick Test

1. What are fixed costs?

2. What are variable costs?

3. Give one example of a fixed cost and one example of a variable cost.

4. What is the break-even point?

Answers 1. Costs which do not change according to output. **2.** Costs which do change according to output. **3.** Fixed – Rent of factory, Variable – cost of raw materials. **4.** The point at which total costs and total revenue are the same.

Cash budgets and cash flow

The cash budget

A cash budget is a financial plan or an estimate into the future. It carefully identifies the projected bills and expenses for the business as well as the projected revenue or income from sales.

A simple Cash Budget is shown below.

Cash Budget of Francisco Rodrigo
For 3 months January–March 2006

	January (£)	February (£)	March (£)
Opening Balance	500	2400	5000
Cash In			
Sales	13000	14700	15500
	13500	**17100**	**20500**
Cash Out			
Purchases	9000	10000	12000
Wages	700	700	700
Rent	800	800	800
Heating and Lighting	600	600	600
Purchase of Machine	0	0	8000
	11100	**12100**	**22100**
Closing Balance	2400	5000	(1600)

From this cash budget it can be seen that the closing balance is (1600). This means there is a negative balance of £1600. Although it is only a projection into the future, this may happen if the owner of the business does not take some action.

The owner of the business will have to decide where to obtain the necessary funds in order for the business to survive. They may ask for an overdraft or a loan from the bank or they may decide to cut back on some expenses.

Top Tip
A negative balance on a cash budget is an indication that the business will be short of cash at some point in the future.

Cash flow

Cash flow is the way in which cash comes into and goes out of the business. Cash is received from customers when they buy goods. Some customers pay straight away, other customers are given one or two months to pay their bills. At the same time the business has bills to pay, such as rent, telephone, wages, electricity, etc. There has to be enough cash coming in at the right time for the business to be able to pay these bills. If there is too big a gap between cash coming in and bills to be paid the business will experience cash flow problems. A cash budget is therefore prepared so that these problems can be identified in advance.

Top Tip
Many businesses fail in the first year because they run out of cash. Cash flow has to be planned and managed so that the business can survive and be successful.

Cash flow problems and how to solve them

The cash budget will let the owner or owners of a business see what problems they may have in the future regarding cash flow. If the budget clearly identifies a cash flow shortage then something has to be done about this.

Look at the cash budget below

Peter Simpson Estimated Cash Budget for July–Sept 2002			
	July £	August £	September £
Opening Balance	500	200	100
Cash in			
Sales	3500	3800	6000
	4000	4000	6000
Cash out			
Purchases	2400	2500	4300
Wages	500	500	1100
Rent	600	600	600
Rates	300	300	300
	3800	3900	6300
Closing Balance	£200	£100	£(200)

From this cash budget you can see that the closing balance is minus £200 – an indication that the business is going to be short of cash.

Peter Simpson, the owner of this business, could try and solve his problems in the following ways:-

- getting a loan or overdraft from the bank
- raising extra capital
- cutting back on projected expenses
- asking suppliers or creditors for extra time to pay bills
- spreading the cost of purchases.

Top Tip

Cash flow problems can be solved in a number of different ways, it does not always involve getting a loan from the bank.

Quick Test

1. What is a cash budget?

2. What does a minus balance mean at the end of a cash budget?

3. Give three ways of improving cash flow problems.

Final accounts

What are final accounts?

Final accounts is the name given to the financial statements prepared by a business, usually at the end of the year. Businesses prepare a trading and profit and loss account and a balance sheet. These statements show clearly the overall financial position of the business.

Trading and profit and loss account

Each year a business will prepare a trading and profit and loss account. This is a statement of the financial performance of the business. The account shows the gross profit and net profit made from trading. An example of a trading and profit and loss account is shown below.

Hair at Home Trading, Profit & Loss Account for the period ended 31 March 2006		
	£	£
Sales		35,000
Less: Cost of Sales		
Opening Stock	6,200	
Add: Purchases	12,300	
	18,500	
Less: Closing Stock	4,200	
		14,300
GROSS PROFIT		20,700
Less: Expenses		
Telephone Calls	1,200	
Petrol	1,600	
Advertising	1,000	
Miscellaneous	500	
		4,300
NET PROFIT		16,400

From the account above you can see that the gross profit was £20,700. This represents the profit made from trading, i.e. from Anita Saqid operating as a mobile hairdresser.

The Net Profit was £16,400. This represents the profit she made after deducting all her expenses such as petrol, advertising and telephone bills.

Top Tip

Gross profit is the profit made from buying and selling. Net profit is the profit left after all the expenses of running the business have been deducted.

Balance sheet

A balance sheet is a statement of the assets and liabilities of a business at a particular date in time. It is sometimes called a 'snapshot' of the business. The balance sheet shows the overall value or worth of the business. An example of a simple balance sheet is shown right.

The sections of a balance sheet are explained below:

- **Fixed assets:** These are the assets that the business owns and are expected to last for a long time, such as premises, equipment and machinery. The business usually needs large amounts of cash in order to purchase fixed assets.

- **Current assets:** These are assets owned by the business but are over a shorter term. Current assets include stock, debtors, money in the bank and any cash that the business has.

- **Current liabilities:** These are bills which have to be paid in the short term, such as overdrafts or creditors. Creditors normally expect to be paid within one to two months.

- **Working capital:** This is the amount left after current liabilities have been deducted from current assets. This shows the true cash position of the business. If there are too many liabilities the business will not be able to pay its bills and will run into cash flow problems. This is known as a liquidity problem or more commonly known as the business 'going bust'.

- **Capital employed:** This is the total value of the business after all liabilities have been deducted. This is a real indication of how much the business is worth.

- **Financed by:** This section shows where the money came from in the first place for the business. In this case you can see that the owner originally put £330,000 into the business.

Balance sheet of Jayne Lee Wong 31 December 2006

	000	000	000
Fixed assets			
Premises			200
Machinery			35
Vehicles			24
			259
Current assets			
Stock	55		
Debtors	24		
Bank	35		
Cash	2		
		116	
Less current liabilities			
Creditors		45	
Working capital			71
Capital employed			330
Financed by			
Capital			330

Using final accounts

Using final accounts to make decisions

The reason for preparing final accounts is to enable the business to make decisions and to evaluate their performance. The business will have to ask questions such as:

- What can we do to increase profits?
- What can we do to increase cash flow?
- Do we have enough current assets?
- Is the overall value of the business acceptable?

Answering these questions will lead to important decisions being made such as whether to:

- increase prices
- increase the volume of sales
- sell off stock quickly in order to increase revenue
- reduce expenses such as telephone bills, gas, electricity, etc.
- employ more workers or make some workers redundant.

Calculating and interpreting simple ratios

In order to obtain a clear picture of the overall performance and value of the business the owners may calculate ratios. Ratios are used to compare performance between years or between different businesses.

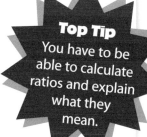

Top Tip
You have to be able to calculate ratios and explain what they mean.

Some of the most common ratios are explained below.

Gross profit %

The formula is $\dfrac{\text{Gross profit}}{\text{Sales}} \times 100$

This ratio shows the gross profit of the business as a percentage of sales.

Net profit %

The formula is $\dfrac{\text{Net profit}}{\text{Sales}} \times 100$

This ratio shows the net profit of the business as a percentage of sales after all the expenses have been deducted.

Return on capital

The formula is $\dfrac{\text{Net profit}}{\text{Capital employed}} \times 100$

This ratio shows the amount the owner of a business receives on capital invested in the business.

Rate of stock turnover

The formula is $\dfrac{\text{Cost of goods sold}}{\text{Average stock}}$

This ratio shows the number of times per year the stock of the business is sold. In some businesses the rate would be high, e.g. foods. In other businesses the rate would be low, e.g. antiques. What is important is that the rate of stock turnover is compared with other similar businesses.

Working capital ratio

The formula is Current assets : Current liabilities

This can be calculated by dividing current assets by current liabilities. This ratio shows the amount of current assets the business has compared to current liabilities. This is a measure of the liquidity of the business. If the ratio is too low, the business may run out of funds and become bankrupt. If the ratio is too high, the business may be wasting money tied up in stock which could go out-of-date and not bring in any future cash. An ideal ratio would be 2:1.

Top Tip
Remember that a business manager is interested in comparisons of ratios from one year to the next or between their own business and other similar businesses.

Quick Test

1. What is the formula for the gross profit %?
2. What is the formula for the net profit %?
3. What is the formula for the rate of stock turnover?
4. What is the formula for the return on capital?
5. What is the formula for the working capital ratio?

Analysing final accounts

Ratio analysis

The calculation of ratios is most effective when a business does this for a few years. The business can then begin to see trends and analyse its performance. Look at the figures for Panik Security Systems Ltd below.

	2002	2003
Gross Profit % Ratio	42%	40%
Net Profit % Ratio	29%	27%
Current Ratio	2:1	1.8:1
Return on Capital Employed	20%	17%

You can see clearly that the ratios changed between 2002 and 2003. Panik Security Systems Ltd will have to investigate why these changes took place in order to find out if there are any further problems with the business. They would continue to do this for the next few years. In this case the ratios have all decreased. They could, of course, increase showing that the business was doing very well.

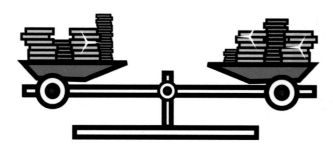

Some possible reasons for ratios changing are shown in the table below.

Ratio	Reasons for increase	Reasons for decrease
Gross profit %	Decreased cost of sales, e.g. discount for bulk buying, reduced prices from suppliers; increased selling prices without an increase in purchase prices	Increased cost of sales, e.g. increased prices from suppliers, wastage of stock, pilfering of stock; decrease in selling price without increase in sales volume
Net profit %	Expenses have been reduced	Expenses have increased
Rate of stock turnover	More stock has been sold; increased sales activity	Slowing down of sales; increase in stock being held; decrease in sales volume
Working capital ratio	Stock figures are too high therefore cash tied up; increased borrowing from bank	Cash balances have reduced; creditors have been paid
Return on capital employed	Net profit may have increased due to reduced expenses or increased advertising	Decrease in net profit due to higher expenses or higher purchase costs

Quick Test

1. Give two possible reasons why gross profit % may increase.
2. Give one possible reason why the net profit % may increase.
3. Give one possible reason why the rate of stock turnover may increase.
4. Give one possible reason why the working capital ratio may decrease.
5. Give one possible reason why the return on capital may increase.

Answers 1. Decreased cost of sales, increased selling prices without increase in purchase prices. **2.** Expenses have been reduced. **3.** More stock has been sold. **4.** Cash balances have been reduced. **5.** Net Profit may have increased due to reduced expenses.

Sources of finance

Where do businesses get their finance from?

All businesses need finance to start up. The amount of finance they need and where they get it from depends on a number of different factors, such as whether the business is a sole trader or a public limited company.

The table below shows the types of finance available to businesses in the UK.

Type of finance	Source of finance
Loan/gift	Family and friends
Savings	Owner of business (sole trader or partners)
Overdraft	Bank, building society
Loan	Bank, building society
Grant	Government, local authority, enterprise company
Grant	Princes Trust
Trade credit (30–90 days usual period for paying for goods)	Creditors or suppliers
Shares	Shareholders in Ltd company or PLC
Debentures (long term loans)	Debenture holders in PLC
Mortgage	Bank, building society
Hire purchase (buying assets over a period of time to spread the costs)	Hire purchase business
Credit cards (using a credit card to delay payment for 5–6 weeks)	Credit card company
Factoring	Factoring company – who buy debts from businesses and give them up to 80% of the value
Loan (small business loan guarantee scheme)	Government

Top Tip

You should understand what source of finance would be suitable in a particular situation for a particular business.

Advantages and disadvantages of sources of finance

The source of finance obtained by a business can bring benefits or drawbacks depending on where the finance is obtained, how long the business gets to pay it back and how much interest is going to be charged. The table below gives some advantages and disadvantages of different sources of finance.

Type of finance	Source of finance	Advantages	Disadvantages
Loan/gift	Family and friends	Can be received quickly; might not have to be paid back; might not be charged interest; no formal interview or papers to complete	Might lead to disagreements in family; not enough funds available for business to start

Type of finance	Source of finance	Advantages	Disadvantages
Savings	Owner of business (sole trader or partners)	Can be accessed quickly; does not have to be paid back; no interest to be charged; no formal interview or papers to complete	No savings to fall back on in future; might not have enough savings for business to start
Overdraft	Bank, building society	Can be accessed quickly; only for a short term so interest not too high	More interest will be added if not paid back in time agreed
Loan	Bank, building society	Can be accessed quickly; can be for many years with fixed interest rate so payments can be budgeted	Have to commit to paying back with interest over a number of years; cannot miss payments or no more finance will be received
Grant	Government, local authority, enterprise company	No interest to be paid; grant usually does not have to be paid back	Conditions usually have to be met which may be difficult for the particular type of business
Grant	Princes Trust	Easy to apply for; encourages 18–25 year olds to start up on their own; grant does not have to be paid back	Conditions may have to be met to receive grant; not guaranteed after application
Trade credit	Creditors or suppliers	Readily available; most businesses offer trade credit; may have received payment for selling goods by time have to pay creditors	Creditor bills can build up if payment not received from customers – can lead to cash flow problems
Shares	Shareholders in PLC	Readily available; shareholders hold limited amount therefore cannot be held liable for all business debts	For PLC shares are limited and therefore not enough to finance the business; shareholders have to be paid dividends on their shares
Debentures (long term loans)	Debenture holders in PLC	Readily available and popular method of company finance; large sums of capital can be raised	Debenture holders must be paid interest whether the company makes a profit or not
Mortgage	Bank, building society	Relatively easy to obtain; can be fixed rate of interest; available over short, medium or long term	Interest charged on mortgage; property can be repossessed if mortgage payments are not kept up
Hire purchase	Hire purchase business	Readily available; easy to organise and obtain; can spread the cost of purchase of assets over a couple of years	Interest charges can be very high; assets are still owned by the finance company until all the payments have been made
Credit cards	Credit card company	Readily available; easy to use; can spread the cost of purchases; credit card companies offer very good deals	Interest has to be paid and can be high; easy to run up debts
Factoring	Factoring company	Cash is received quickly; can help cash flow problems	The full value of the debts are not received, therefore losing profit in the long term
Loan	Small business loan guarantee scheme	Easy to apply; can receive loan quickly; government will meet the costs of the loan if the business fails	Interest has to be paid on the loan.

The external paper

The exam

The external examination covers two elements:

- knowledge and understanding
- decision making.

At Foundation Level the paper lasts for 1 hour.

At General Level the paper lasts for 1 hour 15 minutes.

At Credit Level the paper lasts for 1 hour 30 minutes.

The external paper can ask questions from any of the four Areas of Study of the course.

Knowledge and understanding

Knowledge and understanding (KU) examines what you have learned, so to answer KU questions you have to recall facts. You also have to demonstrate that you understand the knowledge by explaining things. All KU questions should be answered as fully as possible; do not use one word answers.

Decision making

Decision making (DM) examines your ability to look at a business problem and make a decision about the course of action the business should take. They usually have a variety of answers that you can choose from, so you are also often asked to give a reason or justify why you have chosen a particular answer.

The stimulus material or case study

At both General and Credit level all questions begin with a stimulus passage or short case study. This is usually based on a real business or a realistic business. Very often the stimulus material is from the website of a business. You should look at past papers and note the websites of these businesses and have a look at them on the Internet. You may also want to look at any other Scottish businesses that you know, as the papers have included lots of Scottish businesses up until now.

The following steps may be useful in dealing with KU and DM questions.

Step 1	Read the passage or stimulus carefully.
Step 2	Read the questions quickly and get a feeling for the overall topics being answered.
Step 3	Re-read the passage or stimulus and look for keywords or phrases that will help you to answer the questions.
Step 4	Answer each question in turn paying attention to whether it is a KU or DM question.

Top Tip

Read the question very carefully to find out exactly what you have to answer. Underline all the keywords.

Try to use all the space available in the General paper. The bigger the space the more you are expected to write.

In the Credit paper all answers are written in an exam book so there is no restriction on what you can write. Credit answers should be as full as possible. However it is more important to look at the mark allocation and try to write one point for each mark. For a six-mark question you should give at least six sentences in your answer.

Keywords in questions

Both the General and Credit papers use keywords in the questions which help you to work out exactly what is being asked. Some key words and their meanings are given below.

Give	Name some of the key points; there is usually more than one to choose from.
Suggest	Give a possible reason or course of action; there is usually more than one.
Identify	Name the main points.
Describe	Write what you know about the point being asked; give a full account.
Justify	Give reasons for your answer; if the question asks for more than one justification you must make sure your justifications are different.
Explain (the term)	Show that you understand the point being asked by giving details about how and why it is the way it is.
Name and describe	Give the name of the point and then write what you know about it.
Suggest and describe	Give a possible course of action and then describe that course of action.
Suggest and justify	Give a possible course of action and then back up why you have chosen that course of action.
Suggest and give reasons	Give a possible course of action and then give reasons why you have chosen that particular course of action.
Suggest, describe and justify (usually credit only for 6 marks)	Give a possible course of action, then write about the course of action, then say why you have chosen that course of action.

How to pass the written exam

General practice exam question

Exam style question

Using steps 1–4 on page 82 try the General exam question below.

Question: | **Marks**

1. Study the information below and then answer the questions that follow.

JJB Sports plc is the UK's leading sports retailer and now operates about 430 stores across the UK. JJB Sports plc provides goods for customers looking for leisure and casual wear. It regularly carries out market research to ensure that it is providing goods which the customers want.

Adapted from JJB website

(a) Give **one advantage and one disadvantage** to JJB Sports plc of being a public limited company.   2

Advantage _____

_____

Disadvantage _____

_____

(b) Suggest **two possible aims** of JJB Sports plc.   2

1 _____

_____

2 _____

_____

(c) Identify **two stakeholders** of JJB Sports plc.   2

1 _____

2 _____

(d) JJB Sports plc "regularly carries out market research". **Suggest and describe 2 different** methods of **field research** which JJB plc could use.   4

Method 1 _____

Description _____

_____

_____

Method 2 _____

Description _____

_____

_____

(e) JJB Sports plc has decided to employ new staff. Suggest **2** ways of **selecting** employees other than holding an interview.   2

1 _____

_____

2 _____

_____

Credit practice exam question

Exam style question

Using steps 1–4 on page 82 try the Credit exam question below.

Question: **Marks**

2.

Mrs F Smith
143076923   Advantage Card

Boots the Chemist plc is one of the UK's leading companies. Boots offers a wide range of own brand and branded products and services including pharmacy, beauty products, electrical goods, film processing and opticians.

Boots used to rely on traditional market research methods to provide it with some understanding of their customers. Today it knows a great deal more about over 10 million of these customers thanks to its Advantage Card loyalty scheme. The target market segments for the Advantage Card are women, aged 20–45.

The highly successful Advantage Card has been designed to encourage customer loyalty through a range of incentives, promotions and special offers.

Adapted from: IBM Case Study

(a) Other than "Loyalty Cards", suggest and describe **2** market research methods which Boots could use to gather information on their customers. Justify your choices.   6

_____

_____

_____

_____

(b) (i) What is a market segment? _____   2

_____

(ii) Boots targets "women aged 20–45". Identify **2 other** market segments Boots could target. _____   2

_____

(c) Suggest and justify **2** different ways, apart from Loyalty Cards, that Boots could attract customers.   4

_____

_____

_____

_____

Answering in context

The passages are included in each question in order to give a context. This means that you have to try and put yourself in the position of that particular business in order to answer the questions.

Exam style question

Question: **Marks**

For more than a century people have been fascinated with model railways. Hornby has been creating this magic until now – satisfying the demands of its loyal customers. Hornby has traditionally been very **product** led in its approach and is now trying to become more **market led**.

Hogwarts Express, featured in the Harry Potter books and films, has been a hugely successful product for Hornby plc. For younger children, they manufacture a range of Thomas the Tank Engine trains and accessories. The company also produces models of British Rail and Virgin Trains. More recent additions to the Hornby range include the "Virtual Railway" CD-Rom which allows consumers to create their own railway designs on their PCs.

Hornby trains, model railways and accessories are sold by all the major toy retailers in the UK. In addition, a variety of specialist shops stock the products. Customers can also purchase products on-line.

Adapted from: **The Hornby Website**

(b) Suggest ways in which Hornby can "**satisfy the demands**" of its customers.   2

_____

_____

_____

_____

A good answer to this question would be as follows:

Hornby can satisfy the demands of its customers by doing the following:

- Updating its existing train sets or bringing out new train sets.
- Increasing the quality of its train sets.
- Ensuring the safety of its train sets as children will be playing with them.
- Reducing the price of its train sets or having special offers on new ones.
- Offering good customer service, such as a repair service for model trains.
- Selling train sets on their Internet website.
- Having better instructions with the train sets.

Justifications and reasons

CREDIT

The most difficult part of answering questions for many candidates is giving reasons and justifications.

Giving a reason is saying why you have chosen the course of action that you did. Look at the following example:

Exam style question

Question: **Marks**

Microsoft Slashes Price of Xbox

Microsoft announced that it is slashing the price of its Xbox games console just five weeks after the UK launch. The computer giant said its decision to drop the price from £299 to £199 was to compete head-to-head with its two rivals, Sony's PlayStation2 (the market leader) and the Nintendo GameCube. Microsoft denied the decision was due to poor sales of the console since its launch. A company spokeswoman said: "We are very pleased with the Xbox, but don't want the price to prevent customers from the Xbox experience."

Source: Adapted from The Scotsman, 19/04/2002

(d) Choose **2** different ways in which Microsoft could communicate with customers. Justify your choices.   4

_____

_____

_____

_____

You now have to justify your choices:

Microsoft could use written communication, e.g. sending customers a letter, a notice or a leaflet.	Justification: They could do this because written communication methods can be kept as a record for later on. Justification: Written communication methods are easy to read, can give lots of information and are not easily misunderstood.
Microsoft could use visual communication, e.g. TV adverts, pictures in magazines, etc.	Justification: TV adverts will reach a wide audience therefore lots of people will know about Microsoft. Justification: They could do this because pictures are easily understood and easy to remember. Pictures have an impact.
Microsoft could use verbal communication, e.g. radio adverts, telephone calls to customers.	Justification: Radio adverts often have jingles which people remember. Justification: Telephone calls are cost-effective and can answer particular questions very quickly.
Microsoft could use electronic communication, e.g. emails, voicemail, text messages, etc.	Justification: Emails are a very fast and efficient way of communicating across the world; they can also have attachments sent with details of products. Justification: Millions of people now have mobile phones so text messages will get to them directly.

Top Tip
Make sure that you do not use the same justification twice when answering a question.

Be careful with your words

- **Internet:** The Internet is a vast place made up of different components, e.g. the World Wide Web, newsgroups, chatrooms and email. When answering questions on the Internet you have to be specific about which part of the Internet you mean. Just writing the word Internet on its own is not enough. If it is the World Wide Web you mean you must write 'Internet website'.

- **Money:** Money can mean many different things: a source of finance, a bill to be paid, profit or loss, capital. When you are writing about finance be very clear about what you actually mean. Businesses do not make 'money' they make a profit.

- **Advertising:** Advertising takes many different forms: TV, radio, magazines, leaflets, billboards, plasma screens, pop-ups, Internet websites, etc. Do not just write the word advertising on its own as it means very little. Be specific about the method of advertising you mean.

- **Sack the workers:** When faced with a question about employee relations many candidates answer with the phrase 'sack the workers'. This is not usually the first course of action that a business will take and certainly not a Credit level answer. Businesses take a lot of steps before ever considering sacking employees, such as negotiation with trade unions, setting up meetings, working in teams, setting up quality circles, etc.

- **The four factors of production:** The four factors of production are land, labour, capital and enterprise. They are fundamental to every business as a business cannot function without them. At Credit level you will be expected to write about how the factors all come together to form the business.

- **The four Ps of the marketing mix:** The marketing mix is made of the the four Ps: product, price, place and promotion. The way in which the 4 Ps are mixed together determines the success or failure of products and services.

Glossary

assets items owned by a business

balance sheet lists a business's assets and liabilities

channel of distribution how a good or service reaches the customer

customer service developing and maintaining good customer relations

desk research market research using secondary information.

economic stock level the optimum stock level taking account of maximium, minimum and reorder levels

economies of scale the act of getting larger can result in the unit cost of each product falling

entreprenuer a person who combines the factors of production to form a successful business

extension strategy a way of prolonging the product life cycle

field research market research using primary information.

homogenous goods a group of products which are similar

just-in-time a stock control method where stock is provided just when it is needed and **finished goods** are provided directly to the customer

market segment a division of the market

marketing mix prouduct, price, promotion and place

method of distribution how a product is transported to market

product development changing a good or service to make it more attractive to the public.

product life cycle the life of a product through introduction, growth, maturity and decline.

quality assurance ensuring a good or service meets customer requirements

stock control the process of managing the resource of stock

total quality management a method of quality assurance where all aspects of production are geared towards quality

trade discount money off the cost of purchases; offered by a supplier to encourage businesses to buy large quanties (buy in bulk)

Notes

Notes

Notes

Index